Contents

Acknowledgements

My thanks to the Board of Behavioral Sciences and its staff for their continued professionalism and responsiveness.

My thanks to the students who pushed me to embark on this project. I hope it's useful to you.

My thanks to my interns at Caldwell-Clark, who remind me – gently, which I appreciate – that there is a lot more out there to be known.

And my deepest thanks to Angela Kahn, who once again showed that her loyalty and support for her partner far outweighs her desire for sleep or her weariness at seeing the 32nd draft of a section.

You all are awesome.

About the author

Benjamin E. Caldwell, PsyD is an Associate Professor in the Couple and Family Therapy graduate programs in the California School of Professional Psychology at Alliant International University in Los Angeles. He also serves as Adjunct Faculty for California State University Northridge and The Wright Institute in Berkeley, CA. His research papers have been published in the *Journal of Marital and Family Therapy, American Journal of Family Therapy, Journal of Divorce and Remarriage, Journal of Systemic Therapy,* and elsewhere. He regularly gives presentations around the country on legal and ethical issues impacting therapy work. Dr. Caldwell is a California Licensed Marriage and Family Therapist (#42723) and maintains a small private practice specializing in couple relationships.

Other books by Benjamin Caldwell:

Saving Psychotherapy:
How therapists can bring the talking cure back from the brink (2015)

Basics of California Law for LMFTs, LPCCs, and LCSWs,
third edition (2015; prior editions in 2013 and 2014)

Disclaimers

Neither this book, nor any book or test preparation program, can guarantee success on the exam. Of course, your success on the test depends on your ability to learn and recall key information, and apply it in the test setting.

The information in this book is believed to be accurate at the time of printing. However, mistakes can happen, and legal and ethical standards can change quickly. It is the responsibility of each individual therapist to make sure they are remaining current with legal and ethical standards of practice.

Finally, while this book discusses legal requirements for the practice of family therapy, it is intended to be used exclusively in the study process for the California MFT Law and Ethics exam administered by the Board of Behavioral Sciences. **No part of this book should be construed as legal advice or as a substitute for consultation with a qualified attorney.** If you are in need of legal guidance, your professional liability insurer and your professional association may provide legal resources to you at no cost.

Introduction

First thing's first:
You've got this.

The California MFT Law and Ethics Exam is 75 questions over two hours, and it is absolutely a test that you can pass. You've taken a graduate-level course in Law and Ethics that was probably pretty good, and probably not all that long ago. But even if it was a while back or a bit lacking in quality, you can catch up with the current standards fairly quickly.

As licensing exams go, this exam is pretty specific. Later, when it comes time to take the MFT Clinical Exam, you'll need to know the theory and interventions involved in many different models of treatment, you'll need to know crisis intervention, and you'll need to know a wide variety of additional information on effective clinical care *in addition to* knowing the legal and ethical rules governing the profession. But **this first test is just about those legal and ethical rules.** In that way, it's actually a better test all around: It's shorter, it's more clearly geared to public safety, and on your side, it's easier to prepare for.

You've got this.

About this book

This book is meant solely to help you prepare for the California MFT Law and Ethics Exam. It aims to be as efficient as possible in providing the critical, current information you need to know to be successful on the test. There are four main sources for this book:

1) The *AAMFT Code of Ethics*, available at aamft.org
2) The *CAMFT Code of Ethics*, available at camft.org
3) *Basics of California Law for LMFTs, LPCCs, and LCSWs, third edition*, available on amazon.com and at bencaldwell.com
4) California statutes and regulations, a summary of which is available at bbs.ca.gov (complete California law is available at leginfo.legislature.ca.gov)

In addition to those sources, a number of other articles and books were used in the development of this book, as reflected in the endnotes. This is similar to how the test itself is developed: Licensed MFTs use source material common in the field, and develop questions assessing an examinee's knowledge of 121 "knowledge statements" outlined in the Exam Plan the BBS uses for this test.

That Exam Plan is a public document. It's available at bbs.ca.gov/pdf/publications/lmft_2016-law-ethics_exam_plan.pdf . Because it so clearly specifies what kinds of knowledge are needed for the test, the exam plan was also key to the development of this book: **Next to each header in the study guide, you will see small numbers that start with the letter K. These numbers indicate the knowledge statements, in the BBS Exam Plan, that are addressed in that section of the book.** As you'll see, this book covers all 121 knowledge statements necessary for the exam.

That said, I haven't seen the test, so I can't promise that this book goes deeply enough into each knowledge statement that you will be able to answer every possible question the BBS could ask about it. The goal here is efficiency in helping you study, not depth.

Speaking of which, it is worth nothing that this book is not a substitute for a graduate-level Law and Ethics course, or for the textbooks used in such a course. By design, it does not explain *why* the rules governing our profession are the way that they are, nor does it aim to offer detail about how the rules can be changed. This book is not appropriate as a detailed desk reference to California law for clinical practice; for that I would recommend *Basics of California Law for LMFTs, LPCCs, and LCSWs.*

This book also isn't a substitute for a larger text on ethics, or for deep understanding of the ethics codes themselves. For more detailed texts on ethical issues for MFTs, I recommend the following:

- *Issues and Ethics in the Helping Professions* by G. Corey, M. S. Corey, C. Corey, & P. Callanan (9th edition, Brooks/Cole, 2014)
- *Ethical, Legal, and Professional Issues in the Practice of Marriage and Family Therapy* by S. A. Wilcoxon, T. P. Remley Jr., & S. T. Gladding (Updated 5th edition, Pearson, 2013)

Finally, this book isn't a substitute for a test-prep class or the practice exams that test-prep companies offer. It's just a book! It can be used on its own or in conjunction with the workshops, materials, and practice tests that the test-prep companies provide. There are lots of different ways to study for an exam like this, and while none of them are absolutely necessary, they all can be useful. Do what works best for you.

Using this book

The study guide portion of this book is about 60 pages in total, and they're a pretty quick read. Every effort has been made to have this guide include the information you'll need for the test, and nothing more.

There are a handful of citations in the book, which refer to endnotes at the back. Those citations are used for direct quotes, longer explanations that are not critical to your understanding of material for the test, and sources other than the main sources for this book noted on the previous page.

About the Exam

Test basics

The California MFT Law and Ethics Exam is a 75-item, two-hour test. Of those 75 items, only 50 count toward your score; the other 25 items are being tested for possible inclusion in future test cycles. Of course, you have no way of knowing which exam items are scored and which are these experimental items, so it is in your best interest to do the best you can on every item on the test. All questions are four-option, multiple choice questions where you are tasked with choosing the *best* response from the available options.

The test is administered via computer at testing centers around the state, and can be taken at some centers outside the state as well. You can see a complete list of test centers at candidate.psiexams.com . (PSI is an independent company the BBS contracts with for the administration of their exams.) No personal items are allowed into the test centers, and they have strict rules about the clothing that examinees can wear, in order to ensure the security of testing. For example, test centers generally will not allow you to wear or bring any clothing with pockets. Some test centers have lockers where you can store personal items during your test, but some do not.

You will be seated at a workstation where your exam has been pre-loaded into the computer, and you are likely to be given a set of noise-cancelling headphones to use during the test if you wish. (Some examinees find these very helpful for blocking out the sound of other computers in the room, while others simply find them uncomfortable.) The PSI testing centers administer a wide variety of tests for federal and state government agencies as well as private businesses, so it is likely that the other examinees in the testing room with you will be working on several different kinds of tests. Once you've had the opportunity to get settled in and familiarize yourself with the computer you will be using, you follow the on-screen instructions to begin your exam.

Content

Considered as a whole (but without considering experimental items), the test will break down into the following proportions:

Law – 40%
Confidentiality, privilege, and consent – 14%
Limits to confidentiality, including mandated reporting – 16%
Legal standards for professional practice – 10%

Ethics – 60%
Professional competence and preventing harm – 18%
Therapeutic relationship – 27%
Business practices and policies – 15%

The exam is not separated into these sections; you may get questions from various categories in any order. These are merely overall proportions. Still, they can be helpful to know. For example, knowing that ethical issues surrounding the therapeutic relationship make up more than a quarter of the test, you may place an emphasis in your studying on this area.

Scoring

Your score is based on the number of non-experimental items that you answered correctly, out of 50 total. Every item is worth one point – there is no weighting of items based on difficulty, complexity, topic, or any other factor. There is also no penalty for an incorrect response; it is counted as 0 points, just the same as if the item were left blank.

The passing score on the test will vary from one test cycle to the next. Some versions of the test will be more challenging than others, so the BBS conducts careful statistical analysis of each test -- and of every *item* on each test -- to make sure they set the passing score appropriately. For this reason, on the very first version of the test (starting in January 2016), those who take the test in the first few weeks it is available may need to wait up to eight weeks to find out whether they passed.[1] That wait can be anxiety provoking, but it ensures that the passing score will be fair.

Strategy

There are many different test-taking strategies that can help you perform well on the exam. Of course, no test-taking strategy will substitute for having detailed knowledge of the material you're being tested on. But strategies can help maximize your score by helping with items you don't know the answer to, and strategies can help with time and anxiety management.

In general, I defer here to your knowledge of your own strengths and challenges. You probably already know how good of a test-taker you are, and you probably already know what strategies will work best for you. (If you don't, it may be worth it to you to go through a couple of the practice exams offered by test prep companies, and see what strategies help you the most.) Just like for studying, the only bad strategy for test-taking is one that doesn't work for you.

If you're going through a test-prep course or if you already know the strategies that help you the most on exams, you can safely ignore the rest of this section. Here are three strategies specific to this exam that may help you:

1, Take the easy ones first. You can go forward and backward on the test as much as you like. Remember that you have a time limit and that items are not weighted, so a good way to start the exam (and possibly build some confidence) is to go through the whole test, marking the responses you are sure of. Then you can go back and spend more time on those items that need more time to consider. You may find that in a very short time period, you already have half or more of the test completed – and that almost all of those answers are likely correct.

2, Use the process of elimination. Even when you aren't certain of the right response on a particular question, there is a good chance you will be able to identify one or more of the response choices as obviously wrong. Eliminating wrong options greatly increases your chance of getting the question right, even if you're not ultimately sure what the best answer would be. One way of eliminating wrong answers is to notice when a question is asking specifically for a *legal* response or specifically for an *ethical* one – that will allow you to eliminate any response choices that would fall into the other category.

3, Don't get stuck in a rabbit hole. You have 120 minutes to respond to 75 questions. That gives you a little more than 90 seconds per question. If you find yourself getting hung up for more than about 3 minutes on an especially difficult question, move on. Make a mental note (or, if you're using the blank paper provided at the test center, an actual note) of the question you're struggling with and any responses you have ruled out, and then go on to other questions you may be able to answer more quickly.

4, Go ahead and guess. Because there is no penalty for an incorrect response, if there are items you are truly unsure about, it is in your best interest to go ahead and mark your best guess. Use the last few minutes of your test to mark your best guess on all remaining items you aren't sure of. The worst thing you can do is leave an item blank, since that gives you a 0% chance of getting the point for it. Even if you're not able to eliminate any of the response choices from consideration, guessing at it gives you at least a 25% chance of getting it right.

Accommodations

Accommodations are available for examinees with recognized disabilities. If you need accommodations, you will need to arrange for a letter to be sent to the BBS from your health care provider documenting your disability. Common accommodations include a quiet room for testing, or additional time to complete the exam. In rare cases, if it is appropriate, a paper-and-pencil version of the test may be given to examinees with recognized disabilities rather than the computer version. Paper-and-pencil tests need to be scored by hand, which can mean waiting several weeks to find out whether you passed.

At the time of publication for this book, the BBS was not offering additional exam time or any other accommodation for those who speak English as a second language. However, the BBS was considering instituting such an accommodation in the future.

The BBS web site notes that requests for accommodation should be received 90-120 days prior to scheduling an exam. For more information on test accommodations, visit the Testing Accommodations page on the BBS web site at bbs.ca.gov/exams/testing_accomdation.shtml (that's not a typo, it really is "accomdation").

Before the test

Weeks and months before

Because the test is so new to California, it isn't yet clear how long the average MFT will need to study for it in order to pass. The material on which you will be tested is largely consistent with what you would have learned in graduate school, mostly in your Law and Ethics class. So a lot of your preparation will simply be re-familiarizing yourself with that material, and making sure you're caught up on any recent changes that have taken place in the legal and ethical rules governing our profession.

There are, of course, lots of ways to **study the material for the exam.** Do what you know works for you. The law and ethics exam does not contain trick questions, and there is no "secret" way to study. The only wrong way to study is a way that doesn't work for you. If you work well with flash cards, make them. If you're someone who does better with reading and rereading, well, hopefully this book is helpful! The point is, trust your instincts and experience when deciding how to study, and how much. Some will find that an hour a night is all they can handle, while others will want to take several-hour-long blocks of time to study. Similarly, some find it more useful to study with friends or colleagues who are also about to test, while others prefer to study on their own.

The most important thing to do several weeks before the test is to **schedule your exam.** Review the list of test centers at candidate.psiexams.com and choose the one that is most convenient to you. While all of the test centers are designed to have ample parking and similar testing conditions, you might want to consult with others who have recently taken exams at locations close to you. They can prepare you for things like the friendliness (or lack thereof) of test center staff, which can make a big difference in your testing experience. Note that the center you choose to schedule might not be the one that is geographically closest to you; you might find there's one farther away that is easier to schedule on your preferred day and time, or in a neighborhood that you like to visit.

One thing you may find helpful once you have your test scheduled is to **clear your test day of other obligations.** Arrange to take the day off from work, and don't put any other appointments on your schedule. You will want to focus squarely on the test. And once it's over, you will not want to go back to work right away. If you pass, you'll want (and deserve!) a bit of celebration, and if you don't pass, you'll want some time to shake it off.

Another thing to address once your test is scheduled: **tell employers, supervisors, and loved ones about your upcoming test.** Part of this is simply pragmatic: They will need to know that you will be entirely unreachable, even in the event of an emergency, during the time you are taking the test. (Cell phones are, of course, not allowed in the testing room.) But part of it is also to shore up social support: It's good to go into a test knowing that a lot of people are cheering for you, and will be ready to celebrate with you once you pass.

If you're going to use an exam preparation course, it's best to do this a few weeks ahead of the test itself. Specific ideas vary about how far in advance of your test you should put your workshop, but there is general agreement that taking it too close to the test itself may be counterproductive (since you will not have much time to make use of the studying strategies taught in the course, or the materials you picked up there) and that taking it too far in advance can also be problematic (since retention of learned material can fade over time). Depending on your studying and scheduling needs, "a few weeks ahead" is probably a good, loose guideline. Of course, not everyone wants or needs an exam prep course to be ready to take their test or to be successful on it.

The week before

Since you schedule your exam by phone or online, you may not be familiar with the specific location of the test center where you will take the exam. It can reduce anxiety on your test day if you actually **visit the test center** during the week before the test. Try to go to the center in advance around the same time of day that you'll be going for the actual test. This can help you get a feel for traffic, parking, and the like. Based on how long it takes you to get there, you can better plan your actual test day, making sure to give yourself ample time for unexpected delays.

The week before the test is also the time to **wrap up studying**. Hopefully by this time you're feeling confident and ready. If not, it's worth taking an honest look at *why* you're not feeling that way. Is it simple anxiety about the test, or is it a recognition that you don't know the material as well as you should? Anxiety can be managed through relaxation techniques, time with friends, and perhaps a visit to your own therapist. If there are parts of the material you are struggling with, you still have time to shore up your weak points before going in to the exam.

The wrap-up process does involve studying, of course, but **take care of yourself** during this time. There is indeed such thing as too much studying: if it is interfering with sleep, your ability to care for your clients, or your relationships with loved ones, you may find that simply adding on more study time this late in the process will do you more harm than good.

Part of taking care of yourself can be to **adopt a mantra**, or a brief statement you can use repetitively to center yourself and calm your nerves. (A mantra can be part of a larger spiritual or meditation practice, but doesn't have to be.) Here are a few you can choose from, or create one that is a good fit for you:

> *It's just a test. It doesn't define me as a person or as a therapist.*
> *I am ready.*
> *I've had good education, good supervision, and good preparation.*
> *I will be the same therapist after the test that I am before it.*
> *This is a milestone, just one checkpoint on a larger journey.*
> *I will pass.*
> *My friends and family will love me the same no matter what happens.*
> *I know the things I need to know.*

Occasionally, people find that they are really not ready for the test at this point, and may consider rescheduling it for a later date. That's fine, but before taking this step, consider whether it is truly about your readiness, or whether it simply is a reflection of anxiety creeping up on you. If it's anxiety, putting off the test may just mean you repeat the experience a few weeks later.

The day before

The day before the test, spend time reviewing what you know and making sure you have everything ready for the next day. You may want to prepare a checklist of things to do and things to bring to the test with you, such as a photo ID, paperwork confirming the test time and location, and the like. (Remember that most test centers will not allow you to bring personal items into the exam room. Some test centers have lockers you can use to store personal items during the test, but not all do.) Make sure you eat well and get a good night's sleep the night before the exam.

The day of the test

Different people have different ideas about whether it is helpful to do some last-minute studying on the actual day of the test. Do what works best for you. Some find that reviewing material one last time increases their confidence, as they recognize material, get practice questions right, and generally go into the test feeling good about how much they know. Others find that continuing to review at the last minute only increases their anxiety.

The most important thing you can do on the day of the test is to keep your anxiety in check. Have a normal, healthy breakfast. (Food and drinks are not allowed in the testing room, so don't go in on an empty stomach.) Get a pep talk from your partner or a close friend. If you've chosen a mantra, spend time repeating it to yourself.

Before you leave home or work for the test, make sure you have the documents you will need to get in: your photo ID and the confirmation from PSI that includes the date, time, and location of your test. Without these materials, you may not be allowed to take the exam.

After the test

Unless you are testing in the first few weeks of 2016 or have a disability accommodation that requires paper-and-pencil testing, you will find out immediately whether you passed the exam. If you pass, congratulations! You will not need to go through another test until you complete your 3,000 hours of supervised experience for licensure and are sitting for the Clinical Exam.

If you do *not* pass on your first try, you have two options for renewing your intern registration:

1) You can take the test again after a 90-day waiting period, and pass on that attempt. (If you start early, you could attempt the test up to four times in a year.)
2) You can take a 12-hour CE course in California Law & Ethics for MFTs.

If you go the CE route to renew your registration, it is important to note that the whole process will then start over for you in the next year of intern registration. You'll again need to attempt the exam at least once, and if you don't pass the test at some point during the year, you'll again need to take a 12-hour CE course in Law & Ethics to renew the registration.

The BBS will not allow anyone to register with a second intern number, or to sit for the MFT Clinical Exam, until they have passed the MFT Law and Ethics Exam.

> Whether you pass or fail, please let me know how well this book prepared you, and how it can be made even better. Visit **bencaldwell.com/ethics-exam-survey** and complete the quick survey.

Additional information

If you have additional questions about the exam process or requirements, the BBS has made a great deal of information about the updated exam process available on their web site, at www.bbs.ca.gov/exams/exam_news.shtml .

Hopefully this book will be a helpful guide to the information you will need to know for the exam. The more you can integrate the information here into your understanding of clinical work, the better off you will be. Deep knowledge of the information is, of course, likely to be the most important factor in whether you pass the test. But it isn't the only factor.

Many organizations offer test-preparation activities leading up to the exam. Often these materials and courses are incredibly helpful to examinees gearing up for the test. In addition to helping with creative ways to remember the material itself, test prep companies also can offer useful tools for approaching difficult questions and managing test anxiety.

The BBS has been lukewarm toward test-prep companies, out of concern that the companies may suggest there is some "secret knowledge" behind the test when there is not. All of the information you need to know for the exam comes from common materials in the field, including the AAMFT and CAMFT codes of ethics (freely available online), state law and regulation (also freely available online), and the same Law and Ethics textbooks commonly used in MFT graduate courses in the state.

Here we go!

The next section is a summary of information likely to be included on the exam. While the BBS uses 121 knowledge statements, they've been organized here in such a way that should make them easier to study and retain. I've kept the descriptions as brief and simple as possible.

I've divided the next section into seven subsections:

- Parameters of practice
- Documentation & disclosures
- Confidentiality & privilege
- Treatment
- The business of therapy
- Non-therapist roles
- Unprofessional conduct

You can see that some of these correspond with the categories used when considering how the test itself breaks down into different proportions. Given the number of questions about treatment you are likely to encounter, some additional time in that subsection may be warranted.

If you have questions about any of the explanations here, or want to dive deeper on any of the subjects covered in this book, you best first stop is the primary source material used in the development of this book.

You've got this.

Good luck!

What you need to know

Parameters of practice

This section covers the larger boundaries of therapy: What can you do as an MFT, and whom can you treat? What steps are necessary when your personal values or beliefs are getting in the way of quality care? And what are some of the overriding principles of ethical and effective psychotherapy?

Scope of practice K34

Your scope of practice is set in state law. It specifies what someone with an MFT license can legally do. Now, California's MFT scope of practice language is long and a bit obtuse.[2] So rather than quote the whole thing, we'll just talk *about* it.

The MFT scope of practice allows us to work with individuals, couples, families, and groups. (Throughout this book, when you see the word "client," it may refer to an individual, couple, or family.) The MFT scope of practice specifically allows us to use "applied psychotherapeutic techniques," making us psychotherapists. And it allows us to use the training we received in our required coursework – which is key to understanding that MFTs can independently diagnose mental illness.

MFTs can use psychological tests in our work, under two conditions: It has to be with clients we're seeing for therapy, and we have to have adequate training in administering the test.

One of the most important pieces in understanding scope of practice is understanding its limits. MFTs *cannot* provide legal advice, medical advice, or other forms of guidance that are outside the MFT scope of practice. Recommending that a client take a certain medication, for example, would be outside of the MFT scope of practice.

It also is helpful to understand the difference between scope of practice – which is set in state law, and is the same for every MFT in the state – and scope of *competence*, which is based on your specific education, training, and experience. Scope of competence varies by individual MFT, and is primarily an ethical issue. It is discussed later, in the Treatment section.

Self-awareness K46-50

Impairments. Good therapists are keenly aware of their own limitations. If you are struggling with a serious emotional problem, mental or physical illness, or substance use, it can interfere with your ability to provide effective therapy. In addition, if you have a strong emotional reaction to a particular client – perhaps because their struggle mirrors one you have gone through, or because there is something in the client's behavior that you strongly dislike – you may not be able to provide effective services.

Responding to impairments. MFTs need to know the referrals and resources available in the event that the therapist is struggling with an impairment and needs to step away from client care, either temporarily or on a longer-term basis. (Knowledge of appropriate referrals and resources comes up multiple times in the BBS Exam Plan, as it is important in many different sets of circumstances. Obviously, the test will not ask what the closest hospital is, since the same test is being given across the state. But you may be asked about the *kinds* of client referrals and resources that would be most appropriate to a given situation. Referrals should always be appropriate to the level and type of client need.)

For the therapist, obviously seeking treatment is appropriate when the problem is a serious emotional problem, mental or physical illness, or substance use. If the issue is a strong reaction to the client, the MFT should seek supervision and consultation, and consider going to therapy. In whatever time it takes for the MFT to resolve their impairment, protecting the welfare of the client is the highest priority.

Methods to facilitate transfer. In some cases, the impairment of an MFT will lead to their needing to transfer clients to other therapists. If it is possible and appropriate, the MFT may have a termination session with the client, focused on transitioning them to a new provider. The MFT should provide appropriate referrals based on client need. The MFT and client should consider a Release of Information authorizing the transfer of client records to the new provider, and authorizing the old and new therapists to communicate to ensure continuity of care. The MFT should follow up with the new provider to transfer the records and coordinate care appropriately.

Personal values, attitudes, and beliefs. MFTs are ethically prohibited from influencing client decisions on preferred treatment or outcomes based on personal values, attitudes, and beliefs. (Going forward, I'll just say "attitudes" to refer collectively to "values, attitudes, and beliefs.") Obviously, it is important for MFTs to be aware of their own attitudes and how they might impact the therapy process. Therapists allowing for their attitudes to influence them might pathologize the behavior of clients the therapist doesn't like, leading to incorrect diagnoses and poor treatment decisions. They might show bias toward one or more family members, impacting the effectiveness of couple or family work. They might become overly friendly (or overly hostile) with a client. They might place their own belief about a particular problem above current scientific knowledge in the field. Ultimately, the therapist is likely to miss or misinterpret important clinical information, decreasing the likelihood of effective therapy.

Managing the impact of therapist attitudes. So what happens, then, when an MFT becomes aware that they have personal attitudes that are entering into the therapy room? It depends on the nature of what is arising. If the therapist is experiencing judgment or bias toward the client based on personal attitudes, the therapist should carefully consider how those attitudes are impacting treatment. The therapist may seek out supervision or consultation to ensure quality of care, and may go to their own therapy to identify the source of the attitude, working to change it if appropriate. If the therapist attitude is likely to continue interfering in the therapeutic relationship, the therapist may consider referring the client to another therapist – but must be cautious to avoid client abandonment, and to ensure that the referral is not discriminatory in nature. If the therapist refers clients out based on personal attitudes about race, gender, or other protected characteristics, the therapist may be engaging in discrimination.

Client autonomy K61, 85-86

Client autonomy in treatment decisions. Clients have the fundamental right to choose for themselves what kinds of mental health treatment they will participate in. While there are exceptions to this, such as for clients who present an imminent danger to themselves or others and thus can be involuntarily hospitalized, generally speaking, clients can choose their treatment type, treatment provider, and treatment goals as they see fit. (Some goals would be considered inappropriate for therapy, such as a parent bringing their child into therapy in hopes of changing the child's sexual orientation. While a parent is certainly free to pursue this goal, it would not be appropriate for a therapist to attempt to offer this treatment.) Consistent with this principle, clients can also discontinue treatment or change treatment provider at any time.

Collaborative relationship between client and therapist. It is the role of the MFT to *assist* clients in making important life decisions, not to make those decisions for the client. In fact, MFTs are ethically prohibited from making major decisions for their clients, such as decisions about entering or leaving a relationship. Instead we specifically inform clients that such decisions are up to them, and we respect their right to make those decisions as they see fit. In our role as MFTs, we help clients to understand the consequences of various decisions they may be considering, but the ultimate decision-making is up to the client.

This sometimes gets misunderstood as a ban on advice-giving. Many MFTs directly advise their clients, and this can be consistent with models of therapy that place the MFT in a directive, expert role. Even the assigning of homework, which is a common intervention in many therapeutic models, can be considered giving advice, and it is certainly ethically acceptable to suggest that clients try out specific new skills in the week ahead.

Methods to assist client decision-making. There are many ways an MFT can assist a client in decision-making without interfering with the client's autonomy in making those decisions. The therapist can help the client list various courses of action they could take in a difficult time, often expanding the possibilities beyond those the client may see on their own. The therapist can help the client foresee possible consequences of each of the possible courses of action, using current research as well as the therapist's knowledge of the client's specific context. The therapist can assess the client's readiness to act. The therapist can reflect and validate the client's excitement about some possibilities and anxiety about others. Each of these tasks facilitates the client making an important decision on their own, with the therapist's guidance and support.

Best interests of the client K78-80

How legal and ethical obligations impact therapy. Our legal and ethical obligations exist primarily to protect the best interests of clients. They can have the side effect of protecting therapists, by setting clear standards of professional behavior (and thus protecting us from accusations of being unprofessional when we are not), but they fundamentally exist to protect clients *from* us.

Sometimes, our legal and ethical obligations can create an inconvenience for therapist and client alike. Clients may not read every word of a long informed consent document, and therapists may not want to spend time in therapy discussing the limits of confidentiality. However, failing to meet our obligations can place clients at risk in a variety of ways. We fulfill these obligations because it is good for clients, even when it isn't convenient.

Conflicts between legal and ethical obligations. There are many times when there is not a direct conflict between law and ethics, but they set different standards. For example, the law may offer a more strict standard than the ethics codes, or vice versa. In these instances, an MFT should follow the stricter standard, regardless of which set of rules it comes from.

For example, ethics codes require specific written permission from the client before recording sessions. The law is silent on this issue – getting written consent is *allowed*, but not *required*, under the law. In this case, the MFT is obligated to the stricter standard: the ethical requirement.

If there is a direct conflict between the code of ethics and the law – that is, if the law says that you *must* do one thing, while the code of ethics says that you *must* do something that is different from and incompatible with what the law requires – the law wins. MFTs should follow the law, and practice in accordance with the code of ethics to the greatest extent possible.

Conflicts between agency and ethical obligations. It is also common for MFTs to work in settings where ethics codes conflict with workplace policy. Here we see a small disagreement between the major ethics codes for the profession: The AAMFT code requires MFTs to make their commitment to ethical standards known to the organization, and to take reasonable steps to resolve the issue in a way that allows the MFT to practice in keeping with their ethical responsibilities. The CAMFT code simply says that we remain accountable to the standards of the profession even when working as a member or employee of a larger organization. The overriding principle is clear: Agency policy does not provide an excuse for MFTs to ignore their ethical duties.

Consultation and collaboration K43, 65-66

Protecting client rights in consultation and collaboration. Of course, MFTs are encouraged to regularly consult with other professionals and community resources to promote quality client care. It is common for MFTs to collaborate and consult with physicians, teachers, social service providers, and other important persons in a client's life.

When doing such consultations, MFTs respect the confidentiality of their clients. Each member of the treatment unit must give their permission for clinical information to be shared with any outsider, unless an exception to confidentiality applies (see later discussion for more on this).

Effects of concurrent treatment. When done well, concurrent treatment can maximize therapeutic gains. Coordinated care among multiple therapists can mean that family members receive individual therapy to work on their individual concerns at the same time they are receiving family therapy to address relational issues. This may speed improvement by addressing multiple levels of concern at once, and by reducing the homeostatic processes in family systems that can keep individual symptoms locked in place.

Concurrent treatment can also cause problems, however, especially when the multiple therapists involved are not in communication with one another. It is not in the best interests of clients to go to one therapist who encourages the client to create distance from the client's mother, and then to go to another therapist who is working to develop a closer relationship between mother and client.

Ethical guidelines for concurrent psychotherapy. The CAMFT Code of Ethics generally prohibits MFTs from working with a client who is seeing another therapist at the same time, unless there is an agreement in place with the other therapist. This serves the purpose of ensuring coordinated care. (It is worth noting that the CAMFT code uses the word "generally" in this standard, which suggests there are exceptions if the interests of the client are better served by allowing concurrent therapy.)

Diversity and nondiscrimination K81-84

Ethical standards for non-discrimination. The CAMFT and AAMFT codes of ethics both prohibit discrimination in professional services based on the following factors:

- Race
- Age
- Gender
- Gender identity
- Religion
- National origin
- Sexual orientation
- Disability
- Socioeconomic status
- Marital status

The AAMFT code adds health status and relationship status to this list; the CAMFT code adds ethnicity and gender expression.

While the AAMFT code simply says that MFTs "provide professional assistance to persons without discrimination" based on the factors above, the CAMFT code notes that MFTs do not "condone or engage in" discrimination, nor do we refuse services based on any of the above.

Diversity factors in therapy. Virtually any area of difference between client and therapist has the potential to impact the therapy process. While discussions of diversity in the US tend to center on issues of race, ethnicity, and (more recently) sexual orientation, a wide variety of other factors can impact a client's identity and cultural norms. In addition to all of the factors listed in the non-discrimination standards above, therapy can be impacted by differences between client and therapist in urban versus rural setting, educational level, regional identity, and many more.

Ethical standards for providing services to diverse groups. Therapists are ethically obligated to be mindful of all forms of historical and social prejudice, as this prejudice can lead to misdiagnosing clients or pathologizing culturally-accepted behavior. In addition, MFTs "actively strive to identify and understand the diverse cultural backgrounds of their clients by gaining knowledge [and] personal awareness, and developing sensitivity and skills pertinent to working with a diverse client population."[3]

Improving knowledge, skills, awareness, and sensitivity. So what can a therapist do when approached by a client who is different from the therapist in ways that impact the therapy process? While postmodern models of therapy encourage MFTs to allow clients to inform the therapist about the client's life and circumstances, it is likely to be inadequate for a therapist to take no other action to improve their knowledge and skills around the relevant diversity issues. The MFT could:

- Attend a continuing education training on working with the client's population
- Seek consultation or supervision from other therapists who identify as part of, or regularly work with, the client's population
- Seek out greater exposure to the client's population
- Read articles and other literature on the client's population
- Attend their own therapy to address issues of bias

Documentation & disclosures

What we tell clients about therapy is often just as important as the therapy itself. Many of our legal and ethical requirements relate directly to the information given to clients about the therapy process, and the records we keep of the therapy process.

Informed Consent & Disclosures K7, 36, 59-60, 62-64

Informed consent. In order for a client to offer consent that is truly *informed*, they need a reasonable amount of *information* about the treatment process. MFTs have an ethical responsibility to provide clients with appropriate information about the treatment process, so that the client can make an informed decision about whether they want to participate. Because treatment plans and methods can change during therapy, informed consent for treatment is best understood not as a single event but as an ongoing process in therapy.

Facilitating client decisions about treatment. Professional ethics codes require MFTs to provide enough information to clients that the clients can make meaningful choices about whether to start therapy. The nature of this information may vary by therapist and by treatment type. MFTs are specifically obligated to inform clients of the limits of confidentiality, the client's right to autonomy in decision-making (more on that below), and of potential risks and benefits of any new or experimental techniques. MFTs are also encouraged, but not required, to give clients information about the therapist's education, training, theoretical orientation, specialties, and any other information the MFT thinks will be helpful.

Client right to autonomy. Clients have a fundamental right to autonomy, meaning that they alone can choose whether to participate in treatment, what the goals of treatment should be, and what provider to use.

(Some therapy goals might be outside of the MFT's scope of practice or competence, or otherwise inappropriate for therapy. The client remains free to pursue those goals, but the MFT could not provide services to assist the clients toward reaching those goals.) Even when treatment is taking place by court order, clients typically are able to choose their provider. MFTs respect clients' rights to choose whether to start therapy and whether to leave it at any time.

Culturally and developmentally appropriate methods. MFTs should gain consent for treatment in a manner that is culturally and developmentally appropriate. If a client is illiterate, does not read English, or is otherwise unable to make sense of the informed consent document, their signature on it would not truly reflect informed consent. The informed consent process would be better served with a verbal discussion in language that the client can understand. MFTs also should be aware of the possibility that clients may be attending therapy against their wishes, at the demand of a family member; in such instances, it is important for the MFT to determine whether the client is truly providing voluntary consent for treatment.

Clients who can't provide voluntary consent. When a client is unable to provide voluntary consent for treatment, the MFT remains responsible for protecting client welfare. Clients may be unable to voluntarily consent for treatment if they are under the influence of drugs or alcohol, if they have been involuntarily hospitalized as a danger to themselves or others, or if they are a child brought to treatment by their parents, as a few examples.

In these instances, the MFT would still take steps to promote client welfare and facilitate the client's ability to make decisions about treatment to the degree possible. In the case of a client under the influence of drugs or alcohol, the MFT may simply take steps to keep the client safe until the influence of the drug has worn off and the client can voluntarily consent to further treatment. A more thorough informed consent process may take place at that point. If a client has been involuntarily hospitalized, the MFT may remind them of their remaining rights. In the case of a minor, an MFT may utilize an assent agreement, which spells out the purpose, risks, and benefits of therapy in a way that is developmentally appropriate to the child, and allows them to ask questions about the therapy.

You may be wondering why mandated clients have not been part of the discussion here. Generally speaking, clients mandated to treatment by a court or other outside entity retain their right to choose their treatment provider and voluntarily consent to therapy. They may be required by a court to be in therapy, but typically, they don't have to be in therapy *with you*. MFTs working with mandated clients are ethically required to clarify the MFT's role and the limits of confidentiality that will apply to the mandated services. This clarification helps protect client rights, as they can choose whether to go forward in treatment under those rules.

Treatment of minors. In most cases, parents provide consent for the treatment of their child. Anyone under age 18 is a minor under state law, and parents can consent for treatment on their child's behalf. If a minor has two legal parents, then typically either parent can provide consent for therapy for the minor.

If the minor's parents are divorced, consent becomes more complicated. The MFT should request a copy of the custody order to determine which parent's consent is necessary for treatment of the minor. In joint custody, typically either parent can provide consent on their own. If one parent has sole custody, only that parent can provide consent for the minor's treatment. If they refuse or withdraw their consent, the MFT should not treat the minor.[4]

Other caregivers may sometimes bring a minor in for therapy. Another relative who lives in the same home as the minor may provide consent for the minor's treatment if they sign a "Caregiver's Authorization Affidavit." The necessary language of this document is specified in state law.

Minors as young as 12 may be seen *without* parental consent if the minor is mature enough to participate intelligently in treatment. That determination is made by the therapist. In these cases, the therapist still must either make an effort to contact the child's parents, or document why they believe doing so would be harmful. Parents do not have a right to access records for their child if the child consented independently, and parents cannot be forced to pay for services provided to their child without the parents' consent.

Guardians and representatives. When clients are unable to make informed decisions on their own, their guardians and legal representatives have the right and responsibility to make choices on the client's behalf. Most commonly, this happens when a parent or legal guardian consents to the treatment of a minor. However, it can also apply when a client under conservatorship is put into treatment by their conservator, or when a court-appointed *guardian ad litem* seeks treatment for minors involved in a custody dispute. In these and other instances, guardians and legal representatives are responsible for making informed decisions about treatment that will be in the best interest of the client.

Disclosing fees. Under state law, you must inform clients before treatment begins of (1) the fee they will be charged and (2) the basis upon which that fee was computed. If you're confused about that second part, think about the sliding-fee scales used at many training clinics: *Client income* is the basis on which the fee is computed. As another example, some MFTs charge more for couple and family sessions than they do for individual sessions. That's fine, but clients need to know about this before treatment starts. Failure to disclose fees and their basis prior to starting treatment is considered unprofessional conduct.

Documentation K8-13 (except "delivery" in K12), 98-100

Documentation of services. Documentation of therapy is both a legal and ethical requirement. Neither state law nor professional ethical codes define the specific *content* that needs to be in treatment records, and there are a wide variety of formats for things like assessments and progress notes. However, all MFTs are legally required to keep records that are consistent with "sound clinical judgment, the standards of the profession, and the nature of the services being rendered."[5] As we will see, there are some specific things that legally must be documented when they occur, such as client releases of information and specific consent for telehealth services.

Ethical requirements for documentation are more specific. Professional ethical codes demand that treatment and financial records be accurate and adequate. The AAMFT and CAMFT codes of ethics both demand that MFTs document the following:

- Authorization to release confidential information
- Precautions taken regarding multiple relationships
- When client requests for records are refused, the request and reasons for refusal should both be documented
- Specific consent for recording sessions or third-party observation (must be in writing)
- Consent to share confidential and identifiable information in consultations (must be in writing)
- Consent from subjects of evaluations (must be in writing)
- Consent for use of clinical materials in teaching, writing, or presenting, unless client identities are protected

The CAMFT code also encourages, but does not require, MFTs to document their treatment decisions, and any agreements made by members of a group to respect the confidentiality of the group.

Protecting the confidentiality of records. MFTs have an ethical responsibility to store, transfer, exchange, and dispose of records in ways that protect the confidentiality of those records. Methods for protecting the confidentiality of records include:

- Keeping paper records in a secure, locked file cabinet
- Keeping electronic records in a secure, encrypted format
- Carefully controlling who has access to client files
- Shredding paper files to dispose of them

Maintenance and disposal of records. Under state law, records must be maintained for at least 7 years following the last professional contact. If you are working with a minor, records must be maintained for at least 7 years after the minor turns 18.

During the time you are maintaining records, of course you must take reasonable steps to ensure they are secure and confidential. When the time comes that you dispose of old client records, this disposal must also be done in a manner that protects security and confidentiality. An MFT should never simply throw old client files in the trash.

Client access to records. Clients generally have a legal right to access their records, though there are some limitations on this. Unless you believe that the release of records to the client would be harmful, you must comply with their request in a timely manner: Within 5 days if the client simply wants to inspect their records, and within 15 days if the client wants a copy of their record. You cannot refuse a client's request for records simply because they owe you money. You can, however, charge for reasonable costs associated with accessing and copying the client's file, and you can provide a summary of the file rather than the full record if you prefer (this typically must be within 10 days of the client's request). Any client who inspects their record and believes some part of it to be incomplete or incorrect can submit a brief statement to be included in the client file.

If you believe that releasing records to a client would be harmful to them, you may refuse to do so. If you refuse, you need to document the request and your reason for refusal. The client may then request that a third-party professional review the records to see whether that third party agrees with you that the record should not be released.

In the case of couple or family treatment, MFTs get consent from all members of the treatment unit prior to releasing records. This is an ethical requirement.

Release of records to others. Records of treatment can be released to third parties if the client requests it or if there is some other appropriate legal authorization. Most commonly, clients request that their records be forwarded to another therapist or health care provider for continuity of care, or they request that records be provided to their insurance company for the purpose of receiving reimbursement.

When a client requests that their records be released to a third party, this request typically must be in writing, and it must be signed and dated by the client or their legal representative.

There are some instances when a specific authorization to release information is *not* required by law, such as when the information is needed by another provider or health care facility to for the purposes of diagnosis or treatment (in an emergency, for example, there may not be time to gather written authorization), or when the information is required as part of a billing process.

Records are also sometimes released by court order, which is its own form of legal authorization. Subpoenas and court orders are discussed further in the section on Confidentiality & Privilege.

Telehealth. Under California law, therapists who offer services via telemedicine are legally required to first obtain specific consent for telemedicine (the consent can be verbal or in writing) and document this in the cli-client's file. Failure to do so is considered unprofessional conduct. While simply scheduling sessions by phone or email would not qualify as telehealth, providing therapy by phone may qualify, and providing therapy via videoconference certainly would. (Note that throughout this book, "telemedicine" and "telehealth" are used interchangeably.)

HIPAA requirements. Under the Health Insurance Portability and Accountability Act (HIPAA), MFTs covered by the act have specific additional responsibilities to protect the privacy of client records. Among the requirements:

- Designating a privacy official
- Informing clients and staff of privacy policy and procedures
- Disciplining staff members who violate privacy or security rules
- Repairing harmful effects of privacy violations
- Maintaining safeguards against the release of private information
- Having complaint procedures for violations of privacy
- Ensuring confidentiality of electronic health information
- Protecting against threats to information security
- Notifying the department of Health and Human Services of breaches of unsecured health information
- Getting client permission before communicating via unsecured email

Obviously, memorizing that whole list would take a fair amount of brain space. It may work best to simply recall that under HIPAA, MFTs need to have and enforce specific policies to protect the security and confidentiality of health information, and that clients are to be informed of the relevant policies. Most MFTs covered under HIPAA provide clients with a Notice of Privacy Policies that outlines how private information is gathered and used.

There is a specific category of documentation that HIPAA calls "psychotherapy notes," which are a therapist's notes documenting or analyzing conversation with a client that happens in a private psychotherapy session. Within this definition, psychotherapy notes cannot include information like session start and stop times, diagnosis, progress, treatment plans, symptoms, interventions, or prognosis. Psychotherapy notes, as defined under HIPAA, must be kept separate from the rest of the client file and are not considered part of the client record. However, under state law, these records would still be subject to subpoena.[6]

Confidentiality & privilege

Privacy is a cornerstone of the therapeutic relationship. Unless a client can trust their therapist to keep information from therapy private, the client is unlikely to openly share their emotional struggles. MFTs are both legally and ethically required to maintain client confidentiality – that is, to keep all information from therapy private, including even the existence of a therapeutic relationship – unless a specific exception to confidentiality applies. Privacy is so important that even courts cannot usually access information from therapy: Communications between therapist and client are typically considered privileged communications, meaning they cannot be used in court. Again, though, there are several exceptions to this general standard.

Understanding confidentiality K1-2

Laws about confidentiality. Unless a specific exception to confidentiality applies, MFTs are legally required to keep the content of therapy confidential. This means that they do not share any information about clients, including even the existence of a therapeutic relationship, with outsiders.

Laws about disclosure. While confidentiality is the default state, a number of legal exceptions to confidentiality exist. In fact, there are more than 20 instances in state law where confidentiality can or must be broken, and information shared with outside persons or agencies.

Those instances where confidentiality *can* be broken are less relevant, as therapists will typically err on the side of confidentiality unless otherwise required by law. However, there may be instances where a therapist breaks confidentiality because the legally *can* do so and they believe it is in the best interest of the client to do so.

More commonly, though, the times when an MFT breaks confidentiality are limited to those times when the law requires it. These times can be generally broken down into five categories:

- Suspected child abuse
- Suspected elder or dependent adult abuse
- Danger to self or others
- Legal authorization, such as a court order or client release
- Other, less common instances where disclosure is required

The first four categories will be discussed in greater detail below. As an MFT, you need to be keenly aware of them. The fifth category – those less common instances where disclosure is required – includes an investigation by a board, commission, or administrative agency; a lawful request from an arbitrator or arbitration panel; a coroner's investigation of client's death; and a national security investigation. These instances rarely come up in therapy (if I were you, I wouldn't try to memorize those instances). In the event of a national security investigation, MFTs not only are required to turn over client records, but are legally prohibited from informing the client that they have done so.

Exceptions to confidentiality: Child abuse K18-19

Laws about reporting child abuse. MFTs are **mandated reporters** of suspected child abuse when serving in our professional roles. In other words, we are required to report abuse we observe or suspect while in the office, but are not required to report abuse we observe or suspect at the grocery store, at home, or in other non-professional settings.

Your mandated reporting responsibilities are triggered when, in your professional role, you develop **reasonable suspicion** that a minor has been abused. Reasonable suspicion is a specific term with a specific meaning. As the law is written, if another MFT with similar training and experience, when presented with the same information, would reasonably suspect that abuse had taken place, then so should you. You do not need to be certain that the abuse happened in order to reasonably suspect it – for example, you do not need to have personally observed injuries to suspect physical abuse.

There are five types of abuse that must be reported, and one that operates on a permissive reporting standard. The kinds of abuse that *must* be reported are:

- **Physical abuse.** Anyone who willfully causes an injury to a child or engages in cruel or unusual corporal punishment is committing physical abuse.
- **Sexual abuse.** This category includes sexual assault, sexual exploitation, and what the law calls "lewd and lascivious acts." When minors engage in consensual vaginal intercourse, the therapist must consider their ages: If one partner is 14 years old or older, and the other is under 14, the therapist must report. Also, if one partner is under 16 and the other is 21 or older, the therapist must report. Otherwise, the therapist should consider the age and maturational levels of the partners in assessing their capacity to consent and the nature of the relationship (i.e., is it exploitive or otherwise abusive) when deciding whether to report. When minors consensually engage in oral sex, anal sex, or object penetration, the current reporting standard is unclear.[7] As such, this is unlikely to appear on your licensing exam. Of course, non-consensual oral sex, anal, object penetration, or intercourse will always be reportable when a minor is involved.
- **Willful harm or endangerment.** Any person causing a child "unjustifiable physical pain or mental suffering," or any caregiver who allows it to happen, is committing child abuse.
- **Neglect.** Even if it happens by accident, children are being neglected if their basic needs for adequate food, clothing, shelter, medical care, or supervision are not being met. A child does not need to have suffered actual harm for a report of neglect to be made. Note that a parent's informed medical choices, including choices to refuse medical treatment based on religious belief, are not neglect.
- **Abuse in out-of-home care.** This is given its own category for reporting purposes. It applies to kids who are physically injured or killed in child-care or school settings.

In addition to those types of abuse, **emotional abuse** operates on a *permissive* reporting standard, which means that you can report this if you choose to, but you are not required to. Children who witness domestic violence are sometimes reported as victims of emotional abuse.

Once you have developed reasonable suspicion, there are specific **timeframes for abuse reporting** that must be followed. You must make a report by phone to your local child protective agency immediately and follow up with a written report within 36 hours. This timeframe does not change for nights, weekends, or holidays.

Indicators of child abuse. Since the reasonable suspicion standard relies on MFTs having a shared understanding of the times when abuse should be reported, it is critical that MFTs are aware of common physical and behavioral indicators of abuse, neglect, and exploitation. While none of these indicators by themselves would lead to a conclusion of abuse, they should lead an MFT to *consider* whether abuse or neglect may be taking place. Common physical indicators include:

- Unexplained bruises
- Unexplained burns
- Unexplained fractures or cuts
- Evidence of delayed or inappropriate treatment for injuries
- Multiple injuries in various stages of healing
- Injury or trauma to genital area
- Sexually transmitted disease
- Pain, swelling, itching, bruising, or bleeding in genital area
- Unattended medical needs
- Consistent hunger or poor hygiene
- Consistent lack of supervision[8]

Notably, the law specifically states that the pregnancy of a minor, in and of itself, is not sufficient grounds to report suspected abuse. This remains true regardless of the age of the minor.

Common behavioral indicators of abuse and neglect include the following. As with all child and adolescent behaviors, a therapist must be especially cautious not to reach premature conclusions on the basis of behavioral indicators alone, as there are a number of potential causes for each of these that would *not* indicate abuse. However, these behaviors should get a therapist's attention:

- Sudden withdrawn behavior
- Self-destructive behavior
- Bizarre explanations for injuries
- Shying away from contact with familiar adults
- Sleep disturbances, including nightmares or flashbacks
- Substance use
- Anger and rage
- Aggressive, disruptive, or illegal behavior
- Frequent absence or tardiness from school or other activities
- Consistent fatigue or listlessness
- Stealing food
- Extreme need for affection
- Extreme loneliness[9]

Exceptions to confidentiality: Elder and dependent adult abuse K14-17

Laws about reporting elder and dependent adult abuse. Under California law, you must report any time you observe, suspect, or have knowledge of elder or dependent adult abuse. An elder is anyone age 65 or older who resides in California. A dependent adult is anyone age 18 to 64 who resides in California and has physical or mental limitations that restrict their ability to carry out normal activities or protect their own rights. Anyone admitted as an inpatient in a hospital or other 24-hour health care facility is, by definition, a dependent adult.

Reportable types of abuse include:

- **Physical abuse, which includes willful over- or under-medication.** Be careful with this, though – an elder reporting that they are in pain does not mean they are being abused. As long as they are being given the correct amount of medication prescribed by their doctor, it would simply call for a referral back to the client's physician to make any necessary adjustments in medication dosage or type. Various forms of sexual abuse are also included here as physical abuse.

- **Financial abuse.** This category is not a form of child abuse, but does apply to elders and dependent adults.
- **Abduction.** Specifically, the law refers to an elder or dependent adult being taken *outside of California*, or prevented from returning, against their will.
- **Isolation.** Elders who are physically restrained from seeing visitors, or who are being prevented from receiving mail, phone calls, or visitors (when the elder wants to see the visitor), are being isolated. In rare instances, a health condition may make limitations on mail and phone calls clinically appropriate, but there should be good medical documentation for such a decision, and other normal contact should not be restricted.
- **Abandonment.** Caretakers accept responsibility for the adults in their care. Abandonment occurs when a caretaker deserts their patient or gives up on their caretaking responsibilities when a reasonable person would not have done so.
- **Neglect, including self-neglect.** This is reportable not so that the elder or dependent adult will be punished, but so that they can be moved to a higher level of care if it is appropriate to do so.

Unlike child abuse laws, elder and dependent adult abuse reporting laws include permissive reporting of any other form of abuse not otherwise defined in the law. This gives an MFT broad latitude to report behaviors that the MFT considers to be abusive or exploitive, even if those behaviors do not fit neatly into any of the categories listed.

Similar to child abuse reporting, you do not need to have heard a direct report of abuse from the victim in order to develop suspicion that abuse has taken place. However, unlike child abuse reporting laws, the laws on reporting elder and dependent adult abuse say that **if you do hear of abuse directly from the victim, you *must* report it.** There is only a very narrow exception, for when the person has been diagnosed with dementia or another form of mental illness that would impact their memory, there is no other evidence of the abuse, *and* the therapist does not believe the abuse occurred.

The **timeframes for reporting** elder or dependent adult abuse changed considerably in 2013, becoming much more complex. If the abuse did *not* take place in a long-term care facility, then a phone report of the abuse must be made immediately to Adult Protective Services or another local agency authorized to receive adult abuse reports. You then must follow up with a written report within two working days. (If the abuse happened within a long-term care facility, the rules are much more complicated, sometimes requiring duplicate or triplicate reporting, and with varied reporting timeframes.) Recent state law allows for elder and dependent adult abuse reports to be made via Internet, in which case the Internet report should be done immediately, and it replaces both the phone *and* written reports.

Indicators of elder and dependent adult abuse. Common indicators of elder abuse include the following. As is the case with child abuse, it may be inappropriate to conclude that abuse has occurred based solely on an indicator here, as each of these can be caused by incidents that would not qualify as abuse. However, they can raise a therapist's suspicion, and suspicion is the standard for reporting:

- Physical or sexual abuse
    - o Unexplained bruises, welts, or scars
    - o Broken bones, sprains, dislocations
    - o Restraint injuries (marks on wrists)
    - o Unexplained bleeding or injury to genitals
    - o Sexually transmitted disease
    - o Medication over- or under-dosing relative to prescribed amounts
- Abandonment or neglect
    - o Unusual weight loss
    - o Poor nutrition or dehydration
    - o Poor hygiene
    - o Unsanitary or unsafe living environment
    - o Inappropriate clothing (inadequate for cold weather)
    - o Lack of needed medical aids, such as glasses

- Financial abuse
  - Sudden changes in financial status
  - Valuable items or cash missing from residence
  - Unpaid bills when the person has money to pay them
  - Unusual financial activity, or activity the person could not have done (e.g., large withdrawals, ATM withdrawal by hospital inpatient)
  - Sudden appearance of unnecessary goods or services
  - Signatures on checks do not match the person's
- Unusual caregiver behavior (can indicate risk of abuse of any type)
  - Threatening, belittling, or controlling behavior
  - Deserting
  - Burnout (can be evidenced by depression, substance use, poor resilience, or perception that caregiving is burdensome)[10]

It is important for MFTs to be aware that stress and burnout are common among caregivers, and these indicate a risk of abuse, but may also simply mean that the caregiver needs some time away from their responsibilities. Caregiving is difficult, particularly if the person being cared for has severe illness or dementia, is socially isolated, is physically aggressive, or has a history of domestic violence. These factors place the person at greater risk of abuse.

Exceptions to confidentiality:
Danger to self or others K20-25, 75

Identifying need for hospitalization. Under state law, an individual can be hospitalized against their will if they are a danger to others, are a danger to themselves, or are gravely disabled. In such instances, the person is taken to a hospital (or other county-designated facility) for assessment for up to 72 hours, which you may know as a "72-hour hold" or a "5150."[11]

Legal requirements for initiating involuntary hospitalization. When an MFT believes hospitalization is necessary, having a client go voluntarily is usually preferable to the process of involuntary hospitalization. However, if the MFT believes the client has a mental disorder that is causing them to be a danger to themselves or others or is gravely disabled, and the client refuses voluntary treatment, the MFT can begin the process of involuntary hospitalization. In order for a client to be hospitalized against their will, a therapist must be able to cite specific facts (client words, appearance or behaviors) supporting the dangerousness of the client, and the conclusions the therapist drew from those facts. The therapist must then find what the county considers an "eligible professional" to actually write the 5150 application. (Usually a police officer or other person designated by the county serves this role. MFTs can be the eligible professional in some counties, but may need to first go through additional training and certification.) Ultimately, it is up to a professional at the facility designated by the county to receive involuntary holds to determine whether the client is to be involuntarily hospitalized. If that professional agrees, the client can be initially held for up to 72 hours.[12]

Laws about confidentiality in situations of client danger to self or others. Danger to self or others is commonly understood as an exception to confidentiality under the law. The *Tarasoff v. California Board of Regents* case established that danger to a reasonably identifiable victim outweighs client confidentiality. An MFT dealing with a client who poses an imminent danger of serious bodily harm to reasonably identifiable victims must take reasonable steps to resolve the threat, which necessarily include breaking confidentiality. (See "Duty to protect law" below.) When a client is suicidal, the *Bellah v. Greenson* case established that therapists have a responsibility to act to protect the client's safety, and this can involve breaking confidentiality to have the client hospitalized if needed. If a client poses a general danger to others because of a mental health condition, *Tarasoff* does not apply but the therapist still can move to have the client involuntarily hospitalized if needed.

In each of these instances, the MFT breaks confidentiality. The MFT shares information about therapy with others who are involved in resolving the immediate danger. Even in these situations, though, the MFT should share only the information necessary to resolve the immediate threat. Sharing unrelated information about the client's therapy may still be seen as a violation of confidentiality rules.

Methods and criteria to identify when a client poses danger to self or others. Thankfully, there are good, brief ways of assessing clients who may pose a danger to themselves or someone else. Assessments for suicide and violence to others tend to focus on the following factors:

- **Ideation (thoughts).** Is the person actively thinking about harming themselves or someone else? For suicidality, are they romanticizing what their death would be like, for them or for others around them?
- **Planning.** Do they have a specific plan for how they would hurt themselves or someone else? Is it immediate?
- **Intent.** Does the person intend to commit violence? How sure are they? Some clients will fantasize about violence or death without any intent to ever act on these fantasies.
- **Access to means.** How easy would it be to carry out the plan? If they are considering suicide or homicide by gun, is there a gun in the house?
- **Past experience.** Have they attempted suicide or been violent with others before? How? Note that *previous suicide attempts* is the strongest risk factor for future attempts.
- **Protective factors.** What are the reasons the person has not hurt themselves or someone else so far? What would prevent them from suicide or violence in the future?

Demographic factors are also important to keep in mind, though these are not predictive of violence. While suicide is a leading cause of death among adolescents (because other causes of death are not common at this age), statistically, the highest risk for suicide is among the elderly (85+) and the middle-aged (45-64). Men are at higher risk than women. Whites and Native Americans have the highest suicide rates among various ethnic groups.

Duty to protect law. You are probably familiar with *Tarasoff v. California Board of Regents*, the court case that established a therapist's responsibility to act when a client poses an imminent danger of serious bodily harm to a reasonably identifiable victim or victims. In such instances, MFTs have a legal obligation known as "duty to protect." While this is not technically a duty to warn (and in rare instances, it might be inappropriate to warn the intended victim, such as times when doing so might trigger the victim to commit a violent act), the most common methods of protecting potential victims are to notify the victims and law enforcement of the threat. You also have additional protection from liability when you make reasonable efforts to notify both the victim and law enforcement.

The law does *not* require you to report or otherwise act on threats to property. However, threats to property are not considered privileged communication under the law (more on Privilege is below), which CAMFT has interpreted to mean that therapists may share such a threat with law enforcement, the property owners, or others as needed to prevent the danger.

Indicators of intent to harm. Obviously, the strongest indicator of a client's intent to harm someone is when they tell you directly that they intend to harm someone. However, this is not the only indicator a therapist should be aware of. Third-party reports of a client intending to harm another person may be treated similarly to direct reports, if the therapist believes that the third party is a trustworthy reporter. Threats made in writing or by other means may be considered evidence of intent to harm. Indirect statements such as "after today, she won't be around any more" may also be reasonable indicators, based on the MFT's knowledge of the client. Threatening behaviors may also qualify. Clients who are actively using drugs or alcohol may present heightened danger to potential victims.

Exceptions to confidentiality: Legal authorization

Another category of exceptions to confidentiality is triggered when there is an appropriate legal authorization to release information that would otherwise remain confidential. Clients may request that their records be released to a third party, using what is commonly called a Release of Information form. Judges might order the release of records. More information on these instances can be found in the section on "Understanding Privilege" a couple of pages ahead.

Managing confidentiality K73-74

Ethical standards. Both CAMFT and AAMFT have standards for MFTs to specifically inform clients of the limits of confidentiality at the beginning of treatment. (Technically, AAMFT requires such disclosures, while CAMFT simply encourages them.) Of course, this is not the only time when it may be relevant to discuss confidentiality. The AAMFT code notes that therapy may require multiple discussions of confidentiality and its limits.

In addition, throughout the course of therapy there are multiple standards that relate to therapists' responsibility to keep information from therapy private. Consultations, recordkeeping, telemedicine, supervision, teaching/presentation, and preparation for moving or closing a practice are *all* to be done in ways that protect client confidentiality, unless a specific exception applies or the client has granted permission for their information to be shared.

Managing the impact of confidentiality issues. Particularly if an MFT has been required to share information from therapy, a discussion with the client about what information was shared, with whom, and why can help minimize negative impacts on the therapeutic relationship. Such a discussion can also serve to remind the client of the limits of confidentiality, and of the therapist's commitment to protecting the safety of any others involved. For example, if a report of suspected child abuse has been made, the MFT may want to discuss the role that an MFT plays in larger society in protecting vulnerable populations from suspected abuse. Ultimately, a conversation like this can refocus client and therapist on the therapeutic process and (hopefully) repair any harm done to the therapeutic relationship.

Understanding privilege K3-6

Privilege refers to information that can be excluded from court proceedings. Normally, all communications between a therapist and their client are considered privileged communications, meaning that they cannot be used in court. Other examples of communication that is usually privileged include communication between spouses, and communication between an attorney and their client. Privilege is specifically a legal issue, outlined in California law.

This is particularly important in therapy. Clients need to be able to trust that information they have shared with their therapist about mental health symptoms or other emotional problems will not be used against them in court; if that risk exists, clients will understandably be less open with their therapists about struggles in the clients' lives.

Clients generally hold their own privilege. In other words, only the client can waive their own right to privileged communication in most instances. Even when the client is a minor, the client is usually considered the holder of their own privilege, although the minor may not be allowed to waive privilege on their own. A judge may block a minor (or an adult, for that matter) from waiving privilege if the judge believes that waiving privilege is not in the person's best interest. In any case, it is never up to the therapist to determine whether privilege should be waived. That is up to the client, the client's guardian, another court appointee, or a judge.

Release of privileged information. By definition, privileged information cannot be used in a court proceeding. Privileged information may only be released in court if the client has waived privilege, or if a judge has determined that privilege does not apply, based on one or more of the exceptions spelled out in state law (see "Exceptions to privilege" starting on the next page).

Responding to a subpoena or court order. If an MFT receives a subpoena (a legal document requesting that the therapist produce records, appear in court, or both), there are specific steps the MFT is commonly advised to take. These include:

1. **Contact an attorney as soon as possible.** The MFT will benefit from legal guidance throughout this process.
2. **Assess the subpoena for its source and validity.** A subpoena from a judge is a court order – the MFT must obey it. A subpoena from a private attorney is different, and may be fought if the client chooses. Occasionally, an attorney may advise you to object to the subpoena, if there is something wrong with the subpoena itself or how it was delivered.
3. **Contact the client to determine their wishes.** Often, the client will freely authorize the MFT to release the records or appear in court. Sometimes, the client will prefer that the MFT assert privilege on the client's behalf, arguing that the therapist's records or testimony should not be made part of the court proceeding.
4. Unless the client has specifically waived privilege or a judge has determined that privilege does not apply, **assert privilege.** This is considered the appropriate default position for an MFT to take in the absence of other guidance from the client or the court.[13]

Of course, if the client does waive privilege, or if a court determines that privilege does not apply, you must comply with the subpoena.

Exceptions to privilege K26-31

Privilege refers to information that can be excluded from court proceedings. Normally, all communications between a therapist and their client are considered *privileged communications*, meaning that they cannot be used in court. However, there are a number of exceptions to this rule, including six that you may be specifically asked about on your exam:

1) The client makes their mental or emotional condition an issue in a lawsuit.
2) The client alleges breach of duty by the therapist.
3) Evaluation or therapy is taking place by court order.
4) A defendant in a criminal case requested the evaluation or therapy to determine their sanity.
5) The client is under age 16 and is the victim of a crime, and the therapist believes that disclosing that information is in the child's best interests.
6) The therapist was sought out for the purpose of committing a crime or avoiding detection after the fact.

Since each one of these exceptions gets its own Knowledge Statement in the Exam Plan, there is a strong likelihood you will be specifically asked to apply your knowledge of one or more of these.

Treatment

Consideration of legal and ethical responsibilities does not stop at informed consent. Additional legal and ethical responsibilities can arise throughout therapy. While the Law and Ethics Exam is not focused on clinical skills, you may be asked questions that relate to your ability to address treatment issues in a manner that is consistent with legal and ethical responsibilities.

Technology K12 "delivery" portion, 104-106

Telemedicine laws. California and federal laws govern the delivery of services by telehealth. Under state law, clients must be informed about the use of telehealth and give their consent before telehealth services can be provided. The MFT must document that this consent was received.

When delivering services by telehealth, all of the laws regarding scope of practice, client confidentiality, and client rights to information and records continue to apply. MFTs must be particularly cautious when considering using telemedicine to treat clients located outside of California, as a California MFT license only governs services provided to clients located within the state at the time of service.

Ethical standards. The 2015 AAMFT Code of Ethics added a number of specific requirements for therapists providing services via telemedicine. Remember that these obligations operate *on top of* all of the regular ethical requirements for therapy, not in place of them. Therapists providing services via telemedicine are ethically obligated to (these obligations are drawn from both the AAMFT and CAMFT codes, which are largely consistent on this issue):

- Ensure that their use of technology is legally compliant
- Determine that the use of technology is clinically appropriate, considering client needs and abilities
- Inform clients of the risks and benefits of telemedicine, including risks related to confidentiality, clinical limitations, emergency response, and technology failure
- Ensure the security of the communication medium
- Only use telemedicine if the MFT has appropriate training, education, or supervision in the technology being used

Limitations of telemedicine. The use of technology to connect with clients over great distances comes with some natural risks and limitations, some of which are directly addressed in the ethical requirements listed above. Some clients (and some therapists) lack the technical skills needed to use technology in the delivery of mental health services. The technology may not be sufficient for the MFT to pick up on subtle cues that would otherwise be important to assess. The client may need services beyond what the therapist can provide through telemedicine. And of course, there is always the possibility that the technology will simply fail, leaving client and therapist disconnected. While technology may be a suitable method for working with many clients, MFTs must carefully assess whether telemedicine services are appropriate to the client's needs and abilities.

Potential for harm. Taking these concerns a step further, The use of technology in therapy has the potential to harm the client or the therapeutic relationship. Direct harm may come to the client if the MFT is unable to accurately assess the nature or severity of client symptoms, or changes to those symptoms, when seeing a client by phone or online. The client also may be harmed if the therapist is unable to provide needed local resources in an emergency, or if a session taking place by phone or Internet leads to breaches of confidentiality. Even when the client is not directly harmed, the relationship between therapist and client can be damaged when technology is not used responsibly. Clients may perceive that the therapist is not as attendant to their needs, or unable to intervene with them in the ways they would in person. Unless a client is well-motivated for technology-based services, the MFT should carefully consider whether seeing the client in person would be a better fit.

Managing crises K76-77

Ethical obligations for protecting safety. There are no standards in the CAMFT or AAMFT codes of ethics that are specific to the protection of client safety. However, a number of standards are indirectly related. Both codes speak to an MFT's responsibility to advance client welfare, which would include protecting their safety. The AAMFT code makes specific reference to honoring the public trust. And the professions are fundamentally guided by ethical principles of beneficence (doing good), non-malfeasance (avoidance of harm), autonomy, fidelity (honesty and loyalty), and justice.[14] Among these, beneficence, non-malfeasance, and justice all would suggest that an MFT has an ethical responsibility to protect the safety of both clients and the public.

Procedures for managing safety needs. As a general rule, safety needs should be addressed through the least intrusive means necessary to resolve the concern. You wouldn't hospitalize a mildly depressed patient, after all. Here are a few procedures for managing safety needs, ranging from the least to the most intrusive. This is not a complete list, and the options here are not mutually exclusive; it may be appropriate to develop a safety plan *and* increase the frequency of contact.

- **Continue to assess.** In the absence of any specific safety concerns, the therapist would simply continue assessing for safety in future interactions with the client.
- **More detailed assessment.** If a client suggests that their depression is deepening or that their hostility to others is increasing, but does not discuss any specific danger or threat, the therapist should assess the area of concern in more detail.
- **Development of a safety plan.** If a client has a history of safety issues, or is currently showing non-specific safety concerns (for example, a client with mild passive suicidality, but no plan or intent to harm themselves), a therapist may develop a safety plan. This plan lays out specific steps the client can take if their symptoms worsen. Steps usually follow a progression if early steps are unavailable or do not solve the problem. Steps may include con-

tacting loved ones, contacting the therapist, contacting another on-duty therapist, and if these steps are unsuccessful, contacting a 24-hour crisis hotline or calling 911.

- **Increasing frequency of contact.** If you have been seeing a client weekly and you begin to have concerns about their safety, but those concerns do not rise to the level where more immediate intervention is needed, you may ask to see them more often, or for the client to check in by phone more regularly.

- **Refer to a higher level of care.** Clients whose symptoms get worse or who become dangerous during outpatient psychotherapy may be better served through inpatient treatment.

- **Voluntary hospitalization.** Clients who pose an imminent danger to themselves or others and are willing to be assessed and treated voluntarily at a hospital will not be held there against their will. When a therapist is firm with a client that hospitalization is necessary, most clients will choose voluntary hospitalization over involuntary hospitalization.

- **Involuntary hospitalization.** If a client presents a major safety risk and is not willing to be hospitalized, an MFT may initiate the process of involuntary hospitalization. While most MFTs cannot invoke involuntary hospitalization, they can demand that a client be evaluated for a possible 72-hour hold.

Of course, if the safety concern is that the client poses an immediate danger of severe bodily harm to a reasonably identifiable victim, the appropriate procedure would be to notify the victim and law enforcement.

Scope of competence K41-45

Understanding scope of competence. Your scope of competence is defined by your education, training, and professional experience, and so your scope of competence is unique to you and can change over time. Scope of competence is primarily an *ethical* issue, though practicing outside of one's scope of competence is considered unprofessional conduct in state law.

Knowing your own limitations. Just as it is important to be able to identify actions that would be out of the MFT scope of practice, it is also critical to understand when issues come before you that are outside your scope of competence. You can't possibly have training and experience for every possible situation you will encounter in your practice, so acknowledging limitations in your scope of competence is not a weakness. It is good profes-professional behavior.

Need for consultation. When a situation comes up in therapy that is outside of an MFT's scope of competence, a responsible MFT will consult with a supervisor or others to determine what appropriate next steps would be. In many cases, the therapist will work to expand their competence while continuing to work with the client.

Protecting client rights in consultations. While consultations are a regular part of many MFTs' practices, we must be cautious in protecting client rights during such consultations. MFTs only share identifiable and confidential information about a client during a consultation if the client has given specific written consent. Even then, the MFT should only provide the information necessary for the consultation.

Expanding competence. If one's scope of competence is determined by education, training, and experience, then it makes sense that MFTs can expand into new areas of practice, or improve their competence in existing ones, by getting additional education, training, and experience.

Responsibility to remain current. The MFT field is constantly growing and changing, with new treatment models and new scientific developments occurring on a regular basis. The training and experience that make you competent to work with a certain problem today may be considered outdated and inaccurate 10 years from now. MFTs have an ethical responsibility to remain current with new developments in the profession, through the use of education, training, and supervised experience. This is part of the reason why licensed MFTs are required to get continuing education hours in each license renewal cycle.

Working with multiple clients K67-72

Identifying the "client." MFTs are ethically obligated to clarify at the beginning of therapy which person or persons are considered clients, and the nature of the relationship the therapist will have with each person involved in treatment. There is a meaningful difference between a partner or family member *visiting* treatment, where they might offer input or moral support to a client's problem, and being a *part of* treatment, where they may be directly involved in therapeutic interventions.

When a couple, family, or group is considered the client, MFTs have an ethical responsibility to carefully balance the needs of the client with the needs of each individual who is part of the client unit.

Confidentiality. When working with couples or families, confidentiality becomes a key concern. If a client calls between sessions and informs the therapist of a secret, does the therapist have the right to bring that information up in a couple or family session? The AAMFT Code of Ethics takes a default position that MFTs maintain individual confidences unless given specific permission otherwise; the CAMFT code simply acknowledges that MFTs must respect the confidences of their clients, but also notes that the "client" may be more than one person, which brings "unique confidentiality responsibilities."

Most MFTs clarify at the beginning of therapy what the MFT's policy is regarding the holding of secrets. Some MFTs support a no-secrets policy, where individual confidences will not be upheld. Other MFTs prefer a limited-secrets policy, believing this is better for accurate assessment of the couple or family. In either case, it is best for the MFT to have a clear, written policy that each individual participating in treatment has agreed to, and for the MFT to then stick to that policy.

In therapy groups, MFTs educate group members on the meaning and importance of confidentiality, and may ask group members to sign an agreement that they will respect the privacy of the group.

Preserving the therapeutic relationship. Of course, it would not be possible to list all of the factors that can influence the therapeutic relationship in family therapy. Nor is that necessary for an exam about legal and ethical practice. Lots of things can influence the relationship, not all of which are foreseeable. If the MFT keeps client welfare and the preservation of the therapeutic relationship paramount, the MFT will be able to manage most of these factors easily.

Consider two examples: In the first example, an MFT doing couple therapy begins to feel hostility from one of the partners, and is not sure why. The MFT asks the other partner whether it would be ok to meet alone with the hostile partner for a few minutes, and the other partner agrees. During this time, the hostile partner reveals that she is concerned the therapist is siding with her spouse over her. While this was not the MFT's intent, the MFT is able to change behavior moving forward, and offers and apology to the hostile partner.

In the second example, an MFT doing family therapy with a mother, father, and their two adolescent girls assesses that the girls' acting out behavior appears to be related to conflict in the parental subsystem. The MFT discusses with the family the possibility of changing the treatment modality to focus on couple work. While the MFT reminds the family that he enjoys having them all come in, he believes the girls have done their job, and now it is time for him to do his in treating the family's core issue.

In each of these cases, the therapist took steps to support client welfare and the therapeutic relationship, when it would have easily been possible for therapy to go down an unproductive path. An MFT should be able to address therapeutic issues related to their role, the modality of treatment, and the involvement of outsiders openly with clients.

Potential conflicts. When an MFT is providing concurrent therapy to multiple people in the same family system – for example, when the MFT is seeing members of a couple both individually and as a couple – conflicts can quickly emerge. Individuals in the same couple or family may have competing and even incompatible needs. An individual may want to talk with the MFT privately about something they don't want their family to know. More practically, scheduling and costs can become difficult in these situations. MFTs are ethically obligated to carefully consider potential conflicts in these situations, and to take steps to avoid or minimize those conflicts.

Good ways to do so include having a clearly identified "client," maintaining a clear policy on secrets, regularly addressing confidentiality issues, and following a clear treatment plan.

Treatment involving multiple systems or third parties. The AAMFT Code of Ethics encourage MFTs to routinely revisit discussions of confidentiality with clients. This is especially important when treatment involves multiple systems or third parties. In some cases, treating an adolescent systemically may mean involving their teacher, their religious leader, their social worker, and others in the therapy all at once. If these third parties start attending the family's therapy sessions, everyone involved should be clear about what the third parties' roles are in the treatment, and what information may be shared with them. Managing privacy and confidentiality in these situations can be a complex task. Of course, clients should give permission before third parties are brought in to treatment, and should be made aware that they can revoke this permission at any time.

Termination and referrals K89-94

Ethical considerations with interrupting or terminating. There are times when interrupting or terminating therapy is appropriate or necessary even when the goals of therapy have not been reached. You as the therapist may become seriously ill, or need to step away from your practice to care for loved ones. The client may suddenly be called to a military deployment or a new job out of state. The clinic where you are seeing the client may lose its funding. While we all hope these situations will not occur, the reality is that they often do, and an MFT is ethically required to be ready for such abrupt shifts. An MFT also must take appropriate steps when this kind of situation does happen.

MFTs are ethically required to have emergency procedures in place in the event that they become suddenly incapacitated or otherwise unavailable. These procedures may include emergency contact numbers where clients may reach the therapist or others able to take over client care. MFTs are also ethically required to have what is called a *professional will*, which lays out issues like who will take over client care in the event of the therapist's serious injury or death. The person assigned to take over client care must be given access to records so that they can contact clients to let them know of the change; for this reason, many MFTs include an authorization in their informed consent agreement letting clients know that a professional will exists and having clients agree that their records may be forwarded when necessary.

Having these plans in place minimizes the harm that may come to clients when a therapist is suddenly unavailable. However, treatment interruptions or sudden terminations are not always due to something happening to the therapist. Whenever treatment must be interrupted or terminated, regardless of whether it is because of something happening to the client, the therapist, the clinic, or the larger social context, MFTs have ethical responsibilities to *non-abandonment* and appropriate *continuity of care*. Non-abandonment simply means that clients in need of continued services cannot be left to fend for themselves; if treatment with the current MFT must be interrupted or ended, the MFT still has a responsibility to ensure that crisis needs are addressed and that the change in treatment does not result in harm. Continuity of care means that the client is able to receive continued care with another provider appropriate to their needs; most commonly, this means providing referrals that are local to the client, within their financial means, and able to treat the client's specific problem type and severity.

Knowledge of referrals/resources to provide continuity of care. In order to make those referrals when necessary, an MFT must be aware of local resources that can provide consistency of care to clients if therapy is suddenly stopped. Many MFTs maintain referral lists that include local hospitals and crisis resources, low-fee mental health clinics, psychiatrists, other providers whose services are similar to those of the MFT, and additional community resources.

Indicators of need to terminate. The clearest indication that it is time to terminate therapy is, of course, when it is clear that the client has reached their treatment goals, and no new goals have emerged. Even in the absence of having reached the goals of treatment, if a client regularly comes in appearing to no longer be in distress, and sessions are spent on ordinary social conversation, this can indicate that the client is ready to be done with therapy.

Client is not benefiting. Even if the goals of therapy have not been reached, it is appropriate to terminate therapy if it is clear that the client is not benefiting from treatment. Further deterioration of functioning is a clear indication of treatment failure. A lack of improvement in symptoms may or may not indicate a lack of benefit from treatment; if a client entered therapy on a downward trend, simply stabilizing them and keeping them out of hospitalization can be considered a benefit. Ultimately, though, clients should experience a benefit from being in therapy. If, by their own report or by therapist or other observation of client behavior, they are not improving, termination should be considered – with referrals given if symptoms still warrant treatment.

Managing termination. It is generally understood that a good termination process starts at the beginning of therapy, with therapist and client reaching clear agreement on what the goals of therapy are and what improvements will lead to a determination that therapy can end. Discussions of progress toward termination should be a regular part of therapy. Once it is clear that termination is appropriate, a responsible MFT will provide advance notice of termination, and in one or more termination sessions, the MFT will take steps to prevent a relapse of symptoms, recognize the gains the client has made in therapy, and provide appropriate referrals for any additional needed care.

Preventing abandonment or neglect. A termination process that is done too quickly or without appropriate referrals can be considered client abandonment. There may be times when a therapist does need to end therapy abruptly, either due to a medical illness, client job transfer or deployment, or for other reasons. In such circumstances, the MFT (or, in the case of the MFT's illness, someone designated by the MFT) should offer as much advance notice of termination as possible, make appropriate referrals, and follow up to ensure the clients are able to obtain continued services.

The business of therapy

For better or worse, family therapy is a business. The fact that clients (or others) are paying money for mental health services means that MFTs must be responsible in the fees they charge, the disclosures they make, and generally in how the business side of the practice is handled. This section focuses on legal and ethical standards relating to business issues, such as payment for services and advertising.

Setting and collecting fees K107, 109-111

Determining fees. There are many factors you can consider when setting fees, such as a client's income, the fees generally charged for services in your area, your own qualifications, and so on. There are three particular things you *can't* do when determining fees:

- You can't enter into an agreement with other independent practitioners or clinics to set a common fee (or common minimum fee) in your area. This would be a violation of federal antitrust law.
- You can't set different fees based on race, national origin, or any other protected class in anti-discrimination rules.
- You can't set fees that are exploitive (i.e., high fees that take advantage of clients' vulnerability or wealth).

You can raise or lower fees whenever you wish, even for existing clients. You simply need to make sure that your fee changes are within the rules listed above, and that clients have been given adequate notice of the change. There is no specific ethical standard for how long is "adequate."

You have an ethical requirement to inform clients in advance of fees that will be charged for non-therapy services, like copying records, testifying in court, or missed appointments. Remember that you also have a legal requirement to inform clients of fees and their basis prior to starting treatment.

Bartering. Bartering – that is, exchanging clinical services for some other product or service, rather than money – comes with a lot of potential problems. There is risk of exploitation if the market value of the goods or services the client offers as payment exceeds the usual fee the MFT charges. There is also the risk that the therapy relationship will be impacted, if the therapist particularly likes or dislikes the goods or services received, or if they hold strong sentimental value for the client.

In spite of those problems, bartering is not completely prohibited. While MFTs ordinarily do not exchange goods or services from clients in return for the MFT's clinical services – that word, "ordinarily," is used in both the AAMFT and CAMFT codes – it may be ethically acceptable in very limited circumstances. Under the AAMFT Code of Ethics, bartering is *only* acceptable if *all* of these conditions are met:

"(a) The supervisee or client requests it
(b) The relationship is not exploitive
(c) The professional relationship is not distorted; and
(d) A clear written contract is established"[15]

As a general rule, you should not enter into a bartering arrangement with clients. However, under the limited circumstances described above, there may be times when bartering for services is preferable to interrupting or discontinuing treatment.

Collecting unpaid balances. MFTs are within their legal rights and ethical boundaries to collect unpaid balances, and even to use collection agencies or courts when necessary to do so. The ethics codes require that MFTs simply give clients reasonable notice before referring for collection or filing a legal claim. Naturally, the collection agency or court should not be given any clinical information about the client.

Continuation of treatment. The CAMFT Code of Ethics goes so far as to specifically *allow* termination of therapy based on non-payment of fees, so long as the termination is handled in a manner that is clinically appropriate. But when an MFT is unable or unwilling, for any reason, to provide continued care to a client, the MFT must assist the client in making arrangements for continuation of treatment.

Payment for referrals K40, 108

Therapists are both legally and ethically prohibited from accepting any form of payment for referrals. This includes payment from clients as well as payments from the professional you referred the clients to (sometimes called "kickbacks"). The idea here is that referrals should be made *solely* on the basis of what is in the best interests of the client. If you are getting paid for referrals, there is at least the *appearance* of a conflict of interests, as you might make a referral based more on what will financially benefit you than on what will clinically benefit the client.

This issue has become more complex in recent years. In some communities, MFTs participate in "networking groups," which are organizations of professionals who sell a wide variety of goods and services. These professionals join the networking group for the specific purpose of referring potential customers to one another. However, because these groups often operate in a structure where members are rewarded for the referrals they generate (the reward might be the *absence* of a fee that they would otherwise have to pay to participate), MFTs in such groups risk being disciplined for violating the standards against receiving payment for referrals.

Gifts K113-114

While some ethical standards have gotten more strict over time, the standards around giving and receiving gifts have actually grown more flexible. This is due largely to increased recognition of the cultural significance of gifts in many populations. Refusing a small gift may be culturally insensitive. The current AAMFT Code of Ethics requires MFTs to "attend to cultural norms when considering whether to accept gifts from or give gifts to clients." We consider the effect of giving or receiving the gift on the client, and the potential impact of the gift on the therapy process. Interestingly, the current CAMFT code does not mention gifts at all, though the existing standards around non-exploitation would certainly prohibit a therapist from placing the therapist's interests above the client's in deciding whether to accept a gift.

Giving a gift to a client, or accepting a gift from a client, does come with some risks. The client might perceive that the gift changes the nature of their relationship with you to a more personal one. They might hold an expectation that any gift should be reciprocated. They might expect preferential treatment in scheduling or other elements of therapy. In each of these instances (and surely many others you could come up with), the integrity of the therapeutic process can be impacted. Whether you accept or reject a client gift, it is good practice to document your decision-making on the issue. You might consider factors like the cost, nature, and meaning of the gift, how it fits within cultural norms, and its potential impact on therapy.

Third-party reimbursement K37-38, 87-88, 112

Third-party reimbursement rules. Health insurance coverage has expanded significantly since the passage of the Affordable Care Act. Of course, insurance is not the only form of third-party payment; employers, courts, nonprofit organizations, family members, and others may be the ones who are actually paying for client care. MFTs need to be aware of the rules surrounding third-party payment, including the limits on information that can be shared with third-party payers.

Some of the key legal rules regarding third-party payment include:

- **Freedom of choice.** Insurance companies typically must reimburse MFTs alongside other mental health providers. Interns do not have to be reimbursed, though some plans will pay for services provided by interns.
- **Mental disorder only.** Most insurers will only reimburse when there is a diagnosed mental disorder. Some will cover services like couple therapy when there is no diagnosis, but plans are not legally required to do so.[16]
- **Protests and complaints.** Providers can (and generally should) appeal denials of reimbursement. Consumers and providers both can complain to the state about insurance company practices. Depending on the plan, it may be governed by the state Department of Insurance or the Department of Managed Health Care.

One of the most important legal rules regarding third-party reimbursement is the legal prohibition against insurance fraud, which can draw criminal and civil penalties in addition to action against your license. Any falsification of diagnosis, procedure code, amount paid, or any other information for the purpose of receiving insurance payment is insurance fraud.

Parity laws. State and federal law require parity in insurance coverage for mental health. What this means is that insurers cannot use a different deductible or other forms of treatment limitations for mental health that they do not apply to other medical coverage. Co-payments, deductibles, and treatment limitations (like caps on the number of visits or days of coverage) for mental health must be equal to or better than the limits placed on other medical coverage.

Advocacy with third-party payers. Some clients are more able than others to navigate the complex bureaucracy of their insurance company. MFTs have an ethical responsibility to advocate for their clients when necessary and appropriate, so that the clients receive the care they need. MFTs can challenge denials of coverage or denials of payment, and may be able to assist clients in gathering needed information about their coverage or reimbursement processes.

Ethical standards. Insurance fraud is a legal issue. At the same time, MFTs are also ethically obligated to be truthful and accurate in documentation submitted to third-party payers. Additional ethical rules around MFTs' interactions with third-party payers include:

- Disclose to clients what information is likely to be shared with third-party payers
- Explain at the beginning of therapy what the process is for collecting payment in the event that third-party coverage is denied
- Do not withhold records or information simply because you have not yet been paid for services
- Do not limit discussions of treatment alternatives to only those alternatives that will be covered by insurance or other third-party payers

Advertising K39, 95-97

Advertising laws. Essentially any public statement where you suggest that you offer therapy or counseling services to the public would be considered an advertisement – the law is purposefully broad on that. The only exception is church bulletins.

State law is highly specific on the **licensure status** disclosures that need to be included in *any* advertisement of an MFT's services. A licensed MFT needs to include their name, their license number, and their title ("licensed marriage and family therapist") or an acceptable abbreviation ("LMFT" or "MFT"). A registered intern needs to include their name, their registration number, their employer's name, an indication that they are under licensed supervision, and their title ("marriage and family therapist registered intern"). That title can be abbreviated "Registered MFT Intern," but the abbreviation "MFTI" can only be used in an ad if the ad *also* contains the fully-spelled-out title "marriage and family therapist registered intern."

MFTs and interns can advertise themselves as **psychotherapists** and say that they perform psychotherapy, as long as they clearly list their licensure type, something the law already requires anyway.

Therapists can advertise using **fictitious business names**, so long as those names are not misleading and clients are informed of the business owners' names and licensure status before treatment begins.

Ads making any kind of **scientific claims** must be backed by published, peer-reviewed research literature.

Any **fees** included in an advertisement must be exact; you cannot advertise fees in ways like "$95 and up." For this reason, many therapists and clinics choose not to list their fees in their advertising.

It would be unprofessional conduct for any MFT to advertise in a manner that is **false, misleading, or deceptive**. Any claims that would be likely to create unjustified expectations of treatment success are also prohibited by law.

Accurate representation. Ethically, you can only advertise those degrees or credentials you have actually earned, and which are relevant to the practice of marriage and family therapy. If you have a master's degree in family therapy and a doctorate in English, you could not include your doctorate as a professional qualification. Even though you do have a doctorate, it would be a misrepresentation of the credentials you hold relative to your clinical work.

Testimonials. Both the AAMFT and CAMFT Codes of Ethics prohibit seeking testimonials from clients. Clients may feel unduly pressured by such requests. This issue has gotten more complicated in the age of Yelp, Angie's List, HealthGrades, and similar web sites designed for patients to share their experiences with a variety of professionals. Clients sometimes provide testimonials on such sites without being prompted to by therapists. MFTs should be aware that *responding* to any online testimonial may be considered a breach of client confidentiality, even when the client is openly discussing their treatment.

Affiliations. As you would expect, MFTs cannot advertise themselves as being partners or associates of a group that they don't actually belong to. If advertising their membership in CAMFT, MFTs must also indicate their membership type (that is, whether they are clinical, associate, or prelicensed members). These rules come from professional ethical codes.

Non-therapist roles

Therapy isn't the only thing that MFTs do. We also supervise, conduct research, testify in court, teach, and engage in a variety of other professional activities. These activities allow us to use our clinical knowledge to benefit students, supervisees, and the general public in a variety of contexts, but they also come with potential problems, especially when we are providing non-therapy services to people who are also therapy clients.

Multiple Relationships K51-55

A multiple relationship (or "dual relationship" -- the terms are used here interchangeably) occurs any time an MFT has a relationship with a client that is separate from being their therapist. Not all multiple relationships are unethical or illegal, and some can't be avoided, especially in rural areas or in work with more tight-knit communities.

Problematic multiple relationships. Sexual or romantic relationships with a client are expressly prohibited, and discussed in greater detail below. There are some other kinds of multiple relationships that are also expressly prohibited. These include:

- Borrowing money from a client
- Hiring a client
- Joining with a client in a business venture
- Having a close personal relationship with a client

If in MFT engages in any of these same actions with a client's spouse, partner, or family member, this may also be unethical.

Not all multiple relationships can be avoided, especially if you are working in a rural area or with a highly-specific population. It is also true that not all multiple relationships are problematic. If a colleague tells you that you can't see a client because "that would be a dual relationship," they haven't adequately made their case.

Multiple relationships must be carefully examined to see whether they would **impair clinical judgment** or create **risk of client exploitation**. These two considerations are critical to determining whether a multiple relationship can be allowed. If you know and like someone in your community and they ask to see you in therapy, your liking of them would surely influence how you observe them clinically -- in other words, your pre-existing view of them would impair your clinical judgment. (Impairment can mean positive bias as well as negative.) Having a client who coaches your daughter's soccer team could create risk of exploitation, as you could use your knowledge of the client's personal secrets to push for more playing time for your daughter. The fact that you wouldn't actually do this does not eliminate the risk of it, nor does it take away your responsibility to protect clients from that risk.

Even when such risks exist, though, in some cases it may be appropriate to continue with the therapy. If you are the only provider in a rural area, for example, the best interests of the client might be better served by going ahead with therapy. You would then need to take specific actions to reduce the risk of impaired judgment or exploitation.

Managing boundaries. MFTs commonly take steps to ensure the integrity and boundaries of the therapy relationship. This can be especially important when it appears that a client is becoming confused about the nature of the relationship, or is wanting more of a personal or social relationship than what therapy allows.

Some examples of methods for managing boundaries include having a conversation with the client to remind them of the boundaries of therapy; maintaining a clear treatment plan with identified therapy goals; making sure all contact between client and therapist stays focused on therapeutic issues; starting and ending sessions on time; and, when clinically appropriate, limiting contact by phone or other means between scheduled session times.

Potential conflicts of interest. MFTs are ethically obligated to be aware of potential conflicts of interest as they arise. The CAMFT Code of Ethics specifically identifies providing multiple forms of treatment (individual, couple, family, or group) to the same person or family as a potential conflict.

Another potential conflict emerges any time a therapist engages in a non-therapist role, such as consultation, coaching, or behavior analysis, with people who are or have been clients in therapy. In any instance of potential conflict of interests, MFTs have an obligation to clarify their roles, and to distinguish how any non-therapist role is different from therapy. In order to avoid any risk to clients, it may be preferable to refer out for additional services that are different from those for which the therapist was initially hired.

Potentially damaging relationships. Sexual relationships, which are discussed at greater length below, are the best example of a relationship that can be damaging to the client. However, they are not the only example. Other forms of multiple relationships can harm clients directly, through poor care or exploitation, or they may harm clients more indirectly, by reducing their overall confidence in therapy as an effective and worthwhile treatment. Social relationships between MFTs and clients can create confusion about the therapist's role, for example, and can hinder success in therapy by clouding the MFT's clinical judgment.

When multiple relationships can't be avoided. Some multiple relationships are unavoidable. For example, some level of multiple relationship is created any time an MFT gets a new client through a referral from an existing client. Another example occurs in a rural area, where an MFT may have regular interaction with many clients at community gatherings. In these and similar situations, the CAMFT Code of Ethics requires MFTs to "take appropriate professional precautions to ensure that judgment is not impaired and no exploitation occurs."[17] In some cases, the precautions may be as simple as having a conversation with the client to reassure them of confidentiality and clearly separate roles. In other cases, more stringent precautions may be appropriate, like the MFT regularly consulting on the case with a colleague. The AAMFT Code requires that MFTs document the precautions they take.

Sexual relationships K32-33, 56-58

Risk of exploitation. The rules prohibiting sexual contact between therapists and their clients come from a fundamental understanding that because the therapist has power in the therapy relationship, because clients are often emotionally vulnerable, and because the therapy process happens behind closed doors, sexual relationships between therapists and clients are likely to be exploitive and ultimately harmful to clients.

This exploitation does not require sexual *intercourse*, and the legal and ethical standards around sexual relationships are worded in such a way as to include romantically intimate relationships generally, even if there has not been intercourse. A therapist could not avoid discipline by simply telling the licensing board, "But we didn't have sex!"

Intimacy between therapist and client. Sexual conduct -- again, a purposefully broader term than intercourse -- between therapist and client is specifically prohibited under California law. Such contact is also specifically prohibited by both the CAMFT and AAMFT codes of ethics.

Intimacy between therapist and *former* client. For former clients, state law and the CAMFT Code of Ethics each prohibit sexual relationships for two years after the last professional contact. Even after that time, however, the CAMFT Code continues to discourage sexual relationships with former clients, due to the risk that they will be exploitive and harmful to the former client. The current AAMFT Code of Ethics includes a *lifetime* ban on sexual relationships with former clients.

Intimacy between therapist and client's spouse, partner, or family member. State laws about sexual relationships with clients and former clients apply only to the clients themselves. Under ethical guidelines, the prohibition is broader: Therapists *also* may not enter into sexually intimate relationships with clients' spouses or partners. The AAMFT Code of Ethics also prohibits sexual relationships with other known family members of the client's family system.

The *Professional Therapy Never Includes Sex* brochure. If your client informs you that they have had a sexual relationship with another therapist, you are required by law to provide for them the state-authored brochure *Professional Therapy Never Includes Sex*. Failure to provide the brochure is considered unprofessional conduct. Many therapists keep a copy or two of the brochure readily available in their offices; it also can be downloaded and printed when you need it.

Therapy with former romantic partners. Just as it would be unethical to start having sex with a former client (subject to the rules noted above), it would also be unethical to accept a client in therapy who was a former sexual partner. This type of multiple relationship is expressly prohibited by the CAMFT Code of Ethics. Entering into a therapy relationship with the partner or immediate family member of someone with whom the therapist has had a prior sexual relationship is also prohibited. While these situations are not directly addressed in the AAMFT code, it is likely that they would still be considered unethical under the existing rules on multiple relationships.

Research ethics K115-118

Procedures for safeguarding research participants. The most important safeguard for research participants is the process of informed consent. Just as a client should be fully informed of the processes, risks, and potential benefits of therapy, a research participant should be fully informed of the processes, risks, and benefits of their participation in a study. Most studies are overseen by some form of Institutional Review Board, which reviews the protocols and protections the researchers have in place. The MFT codes of ethics also require MFTs to seek the advice of qualified colleagues in designing and conducting research, and to observe appropriate research safeguards.

Necessary disclosures to research participants. Under the CAMFT and AAMFT Codes of Ethics, research participants need to be informed of all "aspects of the research that might reasonably be expected to influence willingness to participate."[18] This would include potential risks or negative effects from participating, and discomfort that the participant might be expected to go through in the study. The AAMFT Code of Ethics also requires that research participants be specifically informed of:

- Purpose of the research
- Expected length of study participation
- Study procedures
- Potential research benefits
- Limits of confidentiality
- Whom to contact with any questions about the research of their rights

Client rights when participating in research. In addition to the right to be informed about the study they are participating in, clients also have the right to decline or withdraw their participation in a study at any time. They also have a right to confidentiality unless they sign a waiver specifically authorizing the release of information from their participation. (If the study is a study involving therapy services, the same limits of confidentiality would apply as ordinarily apply in therapy, and the clients should be informed of this as part of the informed consent process.)

Confidentiality of research data. Unless clients provide a written waiver, MFTs consider any information they learn about a research participant to be confidential, subject to the exceptions to confidentiality outlined earlier. If a participant's family members or others may be able to gain access to a participant's research data, the MFT must explain this possibility at the beginning of the study and share their plan for protecting confidentiality.

Supervision K121

Supervisors have a number of specific responsibilities defined in the CAMFT Code of Ethics. In brief, supervisors are required to:

- Maintain their supervision skills, getting consultation when needed
- Stay up to date in their knowledge of the practice of MFT
- Stay aware of changes to legal and ethical guidelines

- Keep supervisees aware of changes to legal and ethical guidelines
- Address cultural and diversity issues in supervision
- Have clear policies and procedures that are given to supervisees at the beginning of supervision
- Regularly evaluate supervisees, identifying concerns
- Follow the law regarding business and employment practices
- Guide supervisees in getting assistance for problems that might be hurting their work
- Document decisions to let go of supervisees
- Review trainee agreements with universities

Supervisees, meanwhile, also have a number of specific responsibilities defined in the CAMFT Code of Ethics:

- Understand that the clients the supervisee sees are considered clients of their employer
- Know the laws and regulations governing MFT practice and licensing
- Function within the limits of a supervisee's role as defined by law
- Maintain registration as required by law

The AAMFT Code of Ethics further requires that supervisees be specifically informed of the risks and benefits of technology when supervision is going to involve the use of technology.

Legal and other professional roles K101-103

Responsibility to clarify role. MFTs often serve in professional capacities that are different from being a therapist or supervisor. For example, MFTs may serve as custody evaluators, expert witnesses, consultants, or in other roles. When doing so, it is important that MFTs be clear (with everyone: themselves, clients, courts, and anyone else directly involved) about what their role is, how it is different from therapy, and how information from clients may be used and shared with the court or with other professionals.

Conflicting roles. MFTs are responsible for clearly distinguishing between the roles of therapist and evaluator. In the therapist role, an MFT is working clinically with clients to help them achieve therapeutic goals. In an evaluator role, the MFT is to remain objective, simply assessing an individual or family's functioning.

MFTs are specifically discouraged from serving as both therapist and evaluator for the same clients, unless the therapist is required to do so by a court or other legal authority. The most common example of this is custody evaluation: An MFT can be the treating therapist for a family, or be a custody evaluator for them, but not both.

The AAMFT Code of Ethics prohibits MFTs from providing "evaluations for custody, residence, or visitation" for minors that the MFT has treated.[19]

Of course, MFTs who have proper releases of information can inform the court of a minor's or family's progress in therapy. The MFT just needs to be very careful to not include statements that might be considered as evaluative statements related to custody, visitation, or whatever legal proceeding is underway.

Legal proceedings. MFTs who take part in legal proceedings have an ethical responsibility to remain impartial and objective. If your client has given you permission to testify on their behalf in a court case, you are testifying as a fact witness – someone directly involved with one of the parties in the case. Your role is not to advocate on the client's behalf, it is to accurately and objectively answer the questions put before you.

If someone has hired you solely for the purpose of providing expert knowledge to the court, but you do not have any knowledge of the people directly involved in the case, you are testifying as an expert witness. When an MFT testifies as an expert witness, the MFT must base their conclusions on sound clinical judgment and appropriate data, and must acknowledge the limitations of their data and conclusions.

When an MFT gives any professional opinion in a legal proceeding, regardless of what type of witness they role the MFT is in, their testimony must be truthful and not misleading.

Many MFTs have gotten into trouble for writing a letter to a court, or testifying in court, in a way that can be construed as assessing or diagnosing someone the MFT has never actually met. For example, MFTs have been disciplined for making evaluative statements about one parent's fitness for custody when the therapist only ever met with the other parent. The ethical guidelines for MFTs are very clear that MFTs are not to offer opinions about people that the MFT has not personally worked with.

Unprofessional conduct

When a therapist violates professional standards, they are said to have committed unprofessional conduct. The BBS exists to protect the public, not the professionals, and will investigate and (if appropriate) punish unprofessional conduct when it is reported.

Unprofessional conduct laws K35

State law currently defines 28 specific categories of unprofessional conduct.[20] For our purposes, it's most important to know what unprofessional conduct *means*: It refers to **actions taken In a professional role that are below minimum professional standards**. Unlike criminal cases (where you could go to jail) or civil cases (where you might have to pay damages to someone you have wronged), unprofessional conduct rules apply to your professional role. "Unprofessional conduct" refers to those behaviors that can result in action being taken against your license or registration.

The types of conduct defined in state law as unprofessional conduct include the following. The language here is lightly edited from state law, and grouped into categories:

Sexual misconduct
Sexual contact with a client or former client
Committing a sex crime with a minor
Committing a sex crime
Sexual misconduct
Failure to provide Professional Therapy Never Includes Sex

Scope of practice and competence
Performing or offering services outside of scope

Impairment
Impairment due to mental or physical illness or drug dependence
Drug dependence or use with a client while providing services

Confidentiality
>   Failure to maintain confidentiality

Crimes and bad acts
>   Conviction of a crime
>   Committing a dishonest, corrupt, or fraudulent act
>   Discipline by another board or by another state

Fraud
>   Getting or attempting to get a license by fraud
>   Misrepresenting your license or qualifications
>   Impersonating a licensee
>   Aiding someone else's unlicensed activity

Testing
>   Violating exam security or integrity

Supervision
>   Improper supervision of a trainee or intern
>   Violations during or involving required hours of experience

Fees and advertising
>   Failure to disclose fees in advance
>   False, misleading, deceptive, or improper advertising
>   Paying, accepting, or soliciting a fee for referrals

Record-keeping
>   Failure to keep records consistent with sound clinical judgment
>   Failure to comply with client requests for access to records

Telemedicine
>   Violating state telehealth standards

General misconduct
>   General unprofessional conduct
>   Gross negligence or incompetence
>   Intentionally or recklessly causing physical or emotional harm

The category simply called "general unprofessional conduct" allows the BBS to act against you if you violate other law, professional ethical codes, or the professional standard of care while in your professional role. In this way, behaviors that are unethical can also be considered illegal, even if they aren't specifically designated as such in the law.

Now, **you don't need to memorize the entire list above.** Most of it, again, is simply what you would expect (and what is covered in this book). Knowing all of the categories will not be nearly as helpful to you as being able to determine whether a particular behavior qualifies as unprofessional conduct under the law.

When a therapist engages in unprofessional conduct, the client may submit a complaint to the BBS. The BBS then has an investigations unit that assesses the complaint, determines whether it is actionable, and investigates if appropriate. During this time, the MFT has the opportunity to defend themselves. If the MFT is found to have committed unprofessional conduct, the BBS can levy fines, place the MFT on suspension or probation, restrict their practice, and in severe cases, revoke the MFT's license (or registration, in cases involving MFT interns). They also may require other actions, such as regular drug testing, while the MFT is on probation or in order to resolve the disciplinary issue.[21] The disciplinary process is meaningfully different from a criminal trial or a civil lawsuit; the BBS only needs to find *clear and convincing evidence* that a violation occurred to issue a penalty.

Unethical or incompetent colleagues K119-120

MFTs not only need to be able to recognize when their own ability to provide therapy is compromised. We also must be aware of times when a colleague's ability to provide ethical and effective therapy is compromised. **Situations that can impair the integrity or effectiveness of therapy** include multiple relationships (subject to the boundaries previously described); therapist substance abuse, mental illness, or emotional disturbance; bias or discrimination by the therapist; exploitation; and many more.

Unlike some other states, **California does not have any rules allowing practitioners to directly report colleagues who are behaving in unethical or incompetent ways.** So when a client tells you about bad behavior on the part of their previous therapist, you are required to keep this

ormation confidential. Reporting it to the board yourself, or directly con-
onting the colleague, would be an illegal and unethical breach of
confidentiality. If a client grants permission for you to talk with the other
therapist (through a written release of information), you could then address
the other therapist, but it would be important to avoid taking the client's report at face value. There are often two very different sides to such stories,
and therapists treat each other with respect and good faith.[22]

If you learn of another therapist's illegal or incompetent behavior *directly from that therapist*, it can be more complicated. For example, if you
learn that a colleague in your clinic is struggling with an alcohol abuse problem, you could encourage your colleague to seek treatment and to
discontinue seeing clients until the problem is under control. The CAMFT
Code of Ethics encourages MFTs to **offer assistance to colleagues who
are impaired** by substance abuse or mental or emotional problems.[23] Doing
so would certainly be in the best interests of their clients. If the other therapist refuses, though, there is no law or ethical standard that requires or even
allows you to report the colleague to the board, or to take any other action.
In fact, the CAMFT Code of Ethics requires therapists to **respect the confidences of colleagues** when in the context of their professional
relationship.[24]

There is only one situation that calls for specific action on your part
based on another therapist's incompetence: When there has been **a sexual
relationship between that therapist and their client**. In that situation, you
are legally required to provide your client with the state-authored brochure
called *Professional Therapy Never Includes Sex*. Failure to do so is unprofessional conduct, as noted above. Even when you're supplying this
brochure, though, you cannot report the other therapist's conduct to the
board. You can, however, encourage your client to do so.

What is most important in a situation like this is that you take appropriate action to promote the welfare of clients. While you may not report it
yourself when a client tells you that another therapist is behaving unethically
or incompetently, you can (and often should) encourage the client to report
that behavior themselves. You can't *require* the client to make that report –
that would be putting your wishes above the client's – but you can encourage it.

Batting Practice

A few sample questions

The exam itself will not simply ask you to recount facts from the pre-ceding mages. More often, it will ask you to apply and integrate the legal and ethical standards that govern the field. Over the next few pages, you'll get some practice at doing just that.

These questions aren't meant to be a sample test, just a handful of items to give you a sense of how knowledge might be organized and applied to arrive at the right answers here. In each question, assume you are an MFT acting within your professional role. For each question that appears on a right-hand page, just turn the page for the correct answer and rationale. Remember that, as is the case on the test itself, questions may be complex, and they may require careful reading – but they aren't designed to trick. There's a single best answer for each question.

1. Your client is suing her employer, saying that long hours and stressful working conditions caused her anxiety disorder. You receive a subpoena from the employer's attorney, calling on you to produce the client's records and to testify in the case. You contact your client, who asks you not to testify or share her records. You should:

a) Advise her to drop or settle her lawsuit, since you will likely be required to testify and to share her records.
b) Respond to the subpoena by asserting privilege.
c) Waive privilege on the client's behalf, since an exception to privilege applies.
d) Provide no response to the subpoena, since it did not come from a judge.

2. Your friend, who is also an MFT, tells you she has been struggling with a drinking problem since the death of her father six months ago. You should:

a) Report the friend to the BBS, as she is unable to provide quality clinical care.
b) Offer to provide confidential therapy to the friend to protect her clients.
c) Encourage the friend to enter treatment for grief and substance use.
d) Inform the friend's employer that she may not be healthy enough to provide services.

Correct answers and rationales:

1. The correct answer is B. While an exception to privilege does apply here, only the client or a judge can waive privilege. Until you know that either the client has waived privilege or a judge has determined that privilege does not apply, asserting privilege is a good default position. You also can get there by process of elimination: A is an incorrect response because giving the client legal advice would be outside of an MFT's scope of practice; C would be an incorrect response since it is never up to the therapist to determine whether privilege will be waived; and D is an incorrect response because failure to respond to a subpoena is not advisable.

2. The correct answer is C. The CAMFT Code of Ethics guides MFTs to encourage struggling colleagues to receive help for issues that interfere with clinical care. We cannot, however, share this information with the BBS or the employer, as the code requires MFTs to respect the confidences of colleagues. Providing direct treatment to the friend would be an improper dual relationship.

3. You are working with a Latina mother and her 7-year-old son in therapy, when you observe unusual bruises on the boy's face and arms. The bruises seem to be in several different stages of healing. When you ask how he got the bruises, both the boy and his mother refuse to answer You should:

a) Report suspected child abuse.
b) Consider whether physical discipline is common in Latin cultures.
c) Remind the mother of the limits of confidentiality.
d) Ask the child to remove his shirt to inspect his torso for additional injuries.

4. A client asks whether her 75-year-old mother can be part of her therapy. The mother speaks English, but can only read and write in her native language, which you as the therapist are not familiar with. You believe that including the mother in the therapy may be helpful to the client. You should:

a) Have the mother sign your informed consent form and join the therapy.
b) Verbally discuss the process, risks, and benefits of therapy with the mother to help her decide whether to join the therapy, and document the discussion and her response.
c) Refer the mother to a therapist who speaks her native language, and ask the client to sign a Release of Information form authorizing you to speak to that therapist.
d) Ask the mother to teach you her native language so that you can provide all appropriate paperwork in her language.

Correct answers and rationales:

3. The correct answer is A. While the injuries, and both clients' response to the therapist's inquiries, are not a guarantee that abuse has taken place, remember that the therapist does not need to be certain. They just need to reasonably suspect abuse. The location of the injuries, the fact that they are in multiple stages of healing, and the refusal to explain them would amount to reasonable suspicion in almost any MFT's mind. B would not be correct because the abuse reporting standards do not change on the basis of client culture. C is not correct because it would be an insufficient response to what appears to be abuse. D is not correct because this would place the MFT in the role of an investigator, which is not the proper role of a therapist.

4. The correct answer is B. Consent for therapy should be documented, but the client's consent does not need to be in writing. Such a requirement would make it impossible to work with clients who are illiterate. A verbal conversation is the best way to ensure that the mother is truly able to exercise her autonomy and provide informed consent for treatment. A is incorrect because the mother's signature would not mean much on a form she could not understand. C is incorrect because it would not fulfill the request of the client, to have the mother be part of the client's therapy, which you also believe may be helpful. D is incorrect because this would be both time-consuming and a potentially inappropriate dual relationship.

5. Your client has health insurance, but the insurance carrier is refusing to cover the client's therapy because she is seeing you for couple therapy and does not, in your assessment, qualify for a diagnosis of mental illness. You should:

a) Assess the client's ability to advocate on her own behalf with the insurance company.
b) Offer to include an "insurance diagnosis" on the client's paperwork to facilitate coverage.
c) Work with the client to develop an alternative plan for payment.
d) Discontinue therapy.

6. Your new 34-year-old client recently moved to the US from Cuba. Though you are not familiar with Cuban culture, you find yourself strongly liking the client. She is intelligent and confident, and tells you that she is interested in becoming a therapist herself someday. You find it difficult to develop concrete therapeutic goals with her, as it seems the conversation in therapy over the first two sessions has been more social in nature. You should:

a) Learn more about Cuban culture and social norms, to determine whether her behavior is normal.
b) Because the client is from a culture that is not familiar to you, refer her to another therapist as she is outside your scope of competence.
c) Attend therapy to address the pathology that underlies your immediate fondness for the client.
d) Assign the treatment goals you feel would be best, reminding the therapist that she is free to participate or not participate in therapy as she sees fit.

Correct answers and rationales:

5. The correct answer is C. It is legal and fairly common for insurers to provide coverage for therapy only in the presence of a diagnosed mental illness. As such, you will need to work with the client on an alternative plan for payment. A is incorrect because the client's ability to advocate is not relevant; the insurance carrier is within the rules to refuse coverage. B is incorrect as the creation of a diagnosis solely for the purposes of insurance coverage, when the therapist does not believe the client actually qualifies for the diagnosis, would likely be considered insurance fraud. D is incorrect because a sudden discontinuation of therapy could be considered abandonment. While termination due to unpaid fees is ethically acceptable, in this case the client may be able to simply pay out of pocket. Choosing to discontinue therapy would be premature.

6. The correct answer is A. This client offers you the opportunity to expand your scope of competence. Doing so will help you determine whether the social conversation in the first two sessions is a culturally accepted way of building trust and familiarity with a professional, or whether it is more troublesome. B is incorrect because this could be considered discrimination based on national origin. C is incorrect because it is not automatically pathological for you to like a client who is confident and intelligent. While you would want to remain aware of how your biases may be impacting treatment, simply liking a client does not require your own therapy. D is incorrect because it is not up to the therapist to determine the goals of treatment. Goals should be established collaboratively, and to do otherwise may violate a client's right to autonomy

How did you do? If you struggled a bit with these, don't worry. They're a bit complex by design, and may be much more complex than the actual items on the test. If you are interested in taking full-length practice tests, a number of test prep companies make such tests available, and they can help build your confidence going into the exam.

Remember, it's a beatable test.

You've got this.

Good luck!

Appendix:
Exam Plan with Index

Board of Behavioral Sciences

Licensed Marriage and Family Therapist

California Law and Ethics Examination Outline

This document provides detailed information about the LMFT California Law and Ethics Examination, including a description of each content area, subarea and the associated task and knowledge statements. **Each question in the examination is linked to this content.**

Note: The exam outline, including all task and knowledge statements, comes from the BBS outline published online. Page numbers in the following charts refer to where the relevant information can be found within this text.

Breakdown of exam content

Content Area	Percentage
I. Law	**40%**
A. Confidentiality, Privilege, and Consent	14%
B. Limits to Confidentiality/ Mandated Reporting	16%
C. Legal Standards for Professional Practice	10%
II. Ethics	**60%**
A. Professional Competence and Preventing Harm	18%
B. Therapeutic Relationship	27%
C. Business Practices and Policies	15%

I. Law (40%)

This area assesses the candidate's ability to identify and apply legal mandates to clinical practice.

IA. Confidentiality, Privilege, and Consent (14%)

Task Statement	Knowledge Statement	Page
T1. Comply with legal requirements regarding the maintenance/dissemination of confidential information to protect client's privacy.	K1. Knowledge of laws regarding confidential communications within the therapeutic relationship.	49
	K2. Knowledge of laws regarding the disclosure of confidential information to other individuals, professionals, agencies, or authorities.	49
T2. Identify holder of privilege by evaluating client's age, legal status, and/or content of therapy to determine requirements for providing treatment.	K3. Knowledge of laws regarding holder of privilege.	61
	K4. Knowledge of laws regarding privileged communication.	61
T3. Comply with legal requirements regarding the disclosure of privileged information to protect client's privacy in judicial/legal matters.	K4. Knowledge of laws regarding privileged communication.	61
	K5. Knowledge of laws regarding the release of privileged information.	61
	K6. Knowledge of legal requirements for responding to subpoenas and court orders.	62

Task Statement	Knowledge Statement	Page
T4. Comply with legal requirements regarding providing treatment to minor clients.	K1. Knowledge of laws regarding confidential communications within the therapeutic relationship.	49
	K2. Knowledge of laws regarding the disclosure of confidential information to other individuals, professionals, agencies, or authorities.	49
	K3. Knowledge of laws regarding holder of privilege.	61
	K4. Knowledge of laws regarding privileged communication.	61
	K7. Knowledge of legal criteria and requirements for providing treatment to minors.	41
T5. Maintain client records by adhering to legal requirements regarding documentation, storage, and disposal to protect the client's privacy and/or the therapeutic process.	K8. Knowledge of laws regarding documentation of therapeutic services.	44
	K9. Knowledge of laws pertaining to the maintenance/disposal of client records.	45
T6. Respond to requests for records by adhering to applicable laws and regulations to protect client's rights and/or safety.	K10. Knowledge of laws pertaining to client's access to treatment records.	46
	K11. Knowledge of laws pertaining to the release of client records to other individuals, professionals, or third parties.	46
T7. Provide services via information and communication technologies by complying with "telehealth" regulations.	K12. Knowledge of laws regarding the consent to and delivery of services via information and communication technologies.	47, 65
T8. Comply with the Health Information Portability and Accountability Act (HIPAA) regulations as mandated by law.	K13. Knowledge of legal requirements of the Health Information Portability and Accountability Act (HIPAA).	47

IB. Limits to Confidentiality / Mandated Reporting (16%)

Task Statement	Knowledge Statement	Page
T9. Report known or suspected abuse, neglect, or exploitation of dependent adult client to protective authorities.	K14. Knowledge of indicators of abuse, neglect, or exploitation of dependent adults.	55
	K15. Knowledge of laws pertaining to the reporting of known or suspected incidents of abuse, neglect, or exploitation of dependent adults.	53
T10. Report known or suspected abuse, neglect, or exploitation of elderly client to protective authorities.	K16. Knowledge of indicators of abuse, neglect, or exploitation of elderly clients.	55
	K17. Knowledge of laws pertaining to the reporting of known or suspected incidents of abuse, neglect, or exploitation of elderly clients.	53
T11. Report known or suspected abuse or neglect of a child or adolescent to protective authorities.	K18. Knowledge of indicators of abuse/neglect of children and adolescents.	52
	K19. Knowledge of laws pertaining to the reporting of known or suspected incidents of abuse/neglect of children and adolescents.	50
T12. Comply with legal requirements regarding breaking confidentiality to protect the client in the presence of indictors of danger to self/others and/or grave disability.	K20. Knowledge of symptoms of mental impairment that may indicate the need for involuntary hospitalization.	57
	K21. Knowledge of legal requirements for initiating involuntary hospitalization.	57
	K22. Knowledge of laws regarding confidentiality in situations of client danger to self or others.	57

Task Statement	Knowledge Statement	Page
T13. Comply with legal requirements to report and protect when client expresses intent to cause harm to people or property.	K23. Knowledge of methods/criteria to identify situations in which client poses a danger to others.	58
	K24. Knowledge of laws pertaining to duty to protect when client indicates intent to cause harm.	59
	K25. Knowledge of situations/conditions that constitute reasonable indicators of client's intent to cause harm.	59
T14. Comply with legal requirements regarding privilege exceptions in client litigation or in response to breach of duty accusations.	K26. Knowledge of laws regarding privilege exceptions in litigation involving client's mental or emotional condition as raised by the client or client's representative.	63
	K27. Knowledge of laws regarding privilege exceptions in which client alleges breach of duty.	63
T15. Comply with legal requirements regarding privilege exceptions in court-appointed and/or defendant-requested evaluation/therapy.	K28. Knowledge of laws regarding privilege exceptions in court-appointed evaluation or therapy.	63
	K29. Knowledge of laws pertaining to privilege exceptions in defendant-requested evaluation or therapy.	63
T16. Comply with legal requirements regarding reporting instances of crime perpetrated against minor clients.	K30. Knowledge of laws pertaining to the reporting of crimes perpetrated against a minor.	63
	K31. Knowledge of laws regarding privilege exceptions in crime or tort involving minors.	63

113

IC. Legal Standards for Professional Practice (10%)

Task Statement	Knowledge Statement	Page
T17. Comply with laws regarding sexual contact, conduct, and relations between therapist and client to prevent harm to the client and/or the therapeutic relationship.	K32. Knowledge of laws regarding sexual conduct between therapist and client.	86
	K33. Knowledge of legal requirements for providing client with the brochure *Professional Therapy Never Includes Sex.*	86
T18. Comply with legal parameters re: scope of practice.	K34. Knowledge of laws that define the scope of clinical practice.	33
T19. Comply with legal parameters regarding professional conduct.	K35. Knowledge of laws that define professional conduct for licensed practitioners.	93
T20. Disclose fee structure prior to initiating therapy.	K36. Knowledge of laws regarding disclosures required prior to initiating treatment.	44
T21. Comply with legal regulations regarding providing treatment when interacting with third-party payers.	K37. Knowledge of laws and regulations regarding third-party reimbursement.	78
	K38. Knowledge of parity laws regarding the provision of mental health services.	79
T22. Comply with laws regarding advertisement of services and professional qualifications.	K39. Knowledge of laws regarding advertisement and dissemination of information regarding professional qualifications, education, and professional affiliations.	80
T23. Comply with laws pertaining to the payment or acceptance of money or other consideration for referrals.	K40. Knowledge of legal requirements regarding payment or acceptance of money or other considerations for referral of services.	77

II. Ethics (60%)

This area assesses the candidate's ability to identify and apply ethical standards for professional conduct.

IIA. Professional Competence and Preventing Harm (18%)

Task Statement	Knowledge Statement	Page
T24. Consult with other professionals and/or seek additional education, training, and/or supervision to address therapeutic issues that arise outside the therapist's scope of competence.	K41. Knowledge of limitations of professional experience, education, and training to determine issues outside scope of competence.	68
	K42. Knowledge of situations that indicate a need for consultation with colleagues or other professionals.	69
	K43. Knowledge of ethical standards regarding the protection of client rights when engaging in consultation/collaboration with other professionals.	69
	K44. Knowledge of ethical methods of developing additional areas of practice or expanding competence.	69
	K45. Knowledge of the ethical responsibility to remain current in developments in the profession.	69
T25. Consult with other professionals to address questions regarding ethical obligations or practice responsibilities that arise during therapy.	K42. Knowledge of situations that indicate a need for consultation with colleagues or other professionals.	69
	K43. Knowledge of ethical standards regarding the protection of client rights when engaging in consultation/collaboration with other professionals.	38

115

Task Statement	Knowledge Statement	Page
T26. Evaluate therapist's own mental, emotional, or physical problems/impairment to determine impact on ability to provide competent therapeutic services.	K42. Knowledge of situations that indicate a need for consultation with colleagues or other professionals.	69
	K46. Knowledge of problems/impairments that interfere with the process of providing therapeutic services.	34
	K47. Knowledge of referrals and resources to assist in meeting the needs of clients.	34
	K48. Knowledge of methods to facilitate transfer when referrals to other professionals are made.	34
T27. Provide referrals to qualified professionals when adjunctive/alternate treatment would benefit the client.	K41. Knowledge of limitations of professional experience, education, and training to determine issues outside scope of competence.	69
	K43. Knowledge of ethical standards regarding the protection of client rights when engaging in consultation/collaboration with other professionals.	69
	K47. Knowledge of referrals and resources to assist in meeting the needs of clients.	34
	K48. Knowledge of methods to facilitate transfer when referrals to other professionals are made.	34
T28. Manage therapist's personal values, attitudes, and/or beliefs to prevent interference with effective provision of therapeutic services and/or the therapeutic relationship.	K49. Knowledge of the potential impact of therapist's personal values, attitudes, and/or beliefs on the therapeutic relationship.	35
	K50. Knowledge of methods for managing the impact of therapist's personal values, attitudes, and/or beliefs on the client or the therapeutic relationship.	35

Task Statement	Knowledge Statement	Page
T29. Evaluate potential conflict of interest situations to determine the impact on the client or the therapeutic process.	K51. Knowledge of conditions/situations that may impair judgment and/or lead to client exploitation.	83
	K52. Knowledge of methods for managing boundaries and/or professional relationships with the client.	84
	K53. Knowledge of methods for protecting the client and the therapeutic relationship in potential conflict of interest situations.	84
T30. Maintain professional boundaries with client to prevent situations or relationships that may impair professional judgment and/or adversely impact the therapeutic relationship.	K51. Knowledge of conditions/situations that may impair judgment and/or lead to client exploitation.	83
	K52. Knowledge of methods for managing boundaries and/or professional relationships with the client.	84
	K54. Knowledge of relationships that can be potentially detrimental to the client and/or the therapeutic relationship.	85
	K55. Knowledge of methods to prevent impairment to professional judgment and/or client exploitation in situations where dual/multiple relationships are unavoidable.	85
T31. Adhere to ethical guidelines regarding sexual intimacy/contact with prospective, current, or former clients and/or client's spouse, significant other, or family members to avoid causing harm or exploitation of the client.	K56. Knowledge of the potential for client harm or exploitation associated with sexual intimacy/contact between a client and therapist.	86
	K57. Knowledge of ethical standards pertaining to sexual intimacy/contact with clients and/or client's spouse, significant other, or family members.	86
	K58. Knowledge of ethical standards regarding entering into a therapeutic relationship with former sexual partners.	87

IIB. Therapeutic Relationship (27%)

Task Statement	Knowledge Statement	Page
T32. Obtain informed consent by providing client with information regarding the therapist and the treatment process to facilitate client's ability to make decisions.	K59. Knowledge of the ethical responsibility to provide client with information regarding the therapeutic process.	41
	K60. Knowledge of disclosures that facilitate client's ability to make decisions regarding treatment.	41
	K61. Knowledge of client's right to autonomy and to make decisions regarding treatment.	35
	K62. Knowledge of methods for communicating information pertaining to informed consent in a manner consistent with developmental and cultural factors.	42
	K63. Knowledge of the right and responsibility of legal guardian/representative to make decisions on behalf of clients unable to make informed decisions.	43
	K64. Knowledge of methods for protecting client's welfare when client is unable to provide voluntary consent.	42
T33. Evaluate for concurrent psychotherapy the client is receiving with other therapist(s) to determine implications for entering into a new therapeutic relationship.	K65. Knowledge of the effects of concurrent treatment relationships on the treatment process.	38
	K66. Knowledge of ethical guidelines for providing concurrent psychotherapy.	38
	K43. Knowledge of ethical standards regarding the protection of client rights when engaging in consultation/collaboration with other professionals.	38

Task Statement	Knowledge Statement	Page
T34. Address confidentiality and/or therapeutic issues associated with therapist's role, treatment modality, and/or involvement of third parties to protect the client's welfare and/or the therapeutic relationship.	K67. Knowledge of methods to identify the "client" and the nature of relationships when providing therapy to more than one person.	70
	K68. Knowledge of the impact of treatment unit, treatment modality, and/or involvement of multiple systems on confidentiality.	70
	K69. Knowledge of methods to manage factors that impact the therapeutic relationship.	71
	K70. Knowledge of methods to manage potential conflicts when providing concurrent therapy to more than one person.	71
	K71. Knowledge of methods for managing confidentiality and privacy issues when providing treatment to more than one person.	71
	K72. Knowledge of methods for managing confidentiality and privacy issues when treatment involves multiple systems or third parties.	72
T35. Manage the impact of confidentiality/limits of confidentiality on the therapeutic relationship by discussing with the client issues/implications that arise during the therapeutic process.	K73. Knowledge of ethical standards regarding the management of confidentiality issues that arise in the therapeutic process.	60
	K74. Knowledge of methods for managing the impact of confidentiality issues on the therapeutic relationship.	60
T36. Manage the impact of safety and/or crisis situations by evaluating risk factors to protect the client/others.	K75. Knowledge of methods for assessing level of potential danger or harm to client or others.	58
	K76. Knowledge of ethical obligations regarding the management of safety needs.	67
	K77. Knowledge of procedures for managing safety needs.	67

Task Statement	Knowledge Statement	Page
T37. Manage the impact of legal and ethical obligations that arise during the therapeutic process to protect the client/therapist relationship.	K78. Knowledge of the impact of legal and ethical obligations on the therapeutic relationship.	37
	K79. Knowledge of methods for protecting the best interest of the client in situations where legal and ethical obligations conflict.	37
	K80. Knowledge of methods for protecting the best interest of the client in situations where agency and ethical obligations conflict.	37
T38. Manage diversity factors in the therapeutic relationship by applying and/or gaining knowledge and awareness necessary to provide treatment sensitive to client needs.	K81. Knowledge of diversity factors that potentially impact the therapeutic process.	39
	K82. Knowledge of ethical standards regarding nondiscrimination.	39
	K83. Knowledge of ethical standards for providing services congruent with client diversity.	40
	K84. Knowledge of methods to gain knowledge, awareness, sensitivity, and skills necessary for working with clients from diverse populations.	40
T39. Provide treatment that respects client's autonomy and right to make decisions.	K85. Knowledge of the collaborative role between therapist and client in the therapeutic process.	36
	K61. Knowledge of client's right to autonomy and to make decisions regarding treatment.	35
	K86. Knowledge of methods to assist client make decisions and understand consequences.	36

Task Statement	Knowledge Statement	Page
T40. Advocate with and/or on behalf of the client with third party payers to assist client in accessing mental health care.	K87. Knowledge of methods for evaluating client's capacity to advocate on own behalf.	79
	K88. Knowledge of ethical standards pertaining to interacting with third-party payers.	79
T41. Maintain practice procedures that provide for consistent care in the event therapy must be interrupted or discontinued.	K89. Knowledge of ethical considerations and conditions for interrupting or terminating therapy.	72
	K90. Knowledge of referrals/resources to provide consistent care in the event therapy must be interrupted or discontinued.	73
	K48. Knowledge of methods to facilitate transfer when referrals to other professionals are made.	34
T42. Terminate therapy when no longer required or no longer benefits the client.	K91. Knowledge of factors and/or conditions that indicate client is ready for termination of therapy.	73
	K92. Knowledge of factors and/or conditions that indicate client is not benefiting from treatment.	74
	K93. Knowledge of methods for managing the termination process.	74
	K94. Knowledge of methods to prevent client abandonment and/or client neglect.	74

IIC. Business Practices and Policies (15%)

Task Statement	Knowledge Statement	Page
T43. Advertise services by adhering to ethical guidelines regarding the use of accurate representations and information to promote services and/or expand practice.	K95. Knowledge of ethical guidelines regarding the use of accurate representation of qualifications and credentials in advertisements and/or solicitation of clients.	80
	K96. Knowledge of ethical guidelines pertaining to the solicitation of testimonials or statements from clients or others.	81
	K97. Knowledge of ethical guidelines regarding the recruitment of clients through employment and/or professional affiliations.	81
T44. Maintain client records by adhering to ethical guidelines to document treatment and/or protect the client's confidentiality.	K98. Knowledge of ethical guidelines regarding the documentation of therapeutic services consistent with clinical practice.	44
	K99. Knowledge of methods for providing reasonable protection of the confidentiality of client records.	45
	K100. Knowledge of ethical guidelines for releasing client records upon request.	46
T45. Clarify role(s) when acting in a professional capacity other than providing treatment or supervision to avoid confusion, maintain objectivity, and/or protect the therapeutic relationship.	K101. Knowledge of the ethical responsibility to clarify roles when acting in a professional capacity other than providing treatment or supervision.	89
	K102. Knowledge of ethical guidelines regarding engaging in conflicting and/or dual roles.	90
	K103. Knowledge of methods for maintaining impartiality and/or professional integrity when engaging in legal proceedings.	90

Task Statement	Knowledge Statement	Page
T46. Implement policies/procedures that address ethical issues associated with the use of electronic media and technology in the course of providing therapy.	K104. Knowledge of the potential for harm to the client or therapeutic relationship with the use of electronic media in the therapeutic process.	66
	K105. Knowledge of ethical standards for interacting with clients via electronic media.	65
	K106. Knowledge of the limitations and risks associated with electronic means of service delivery.	66
T47. Maintain fee/payment policies that are commensurate with services provided and protect the therapeutic relationship.	K107. Knowledge of methods and conditions for determining fees commensurate with professional services.	75
	K108. Knowledge of prohibited business practices/forms of remuneration for making/accepting client referrals.	77
	K109. Knowledge of the potential for client exploitation or harm that may result from bartering/exchanges for services.	76
	K110. Knowledge of ethical standards pertaining to the collection of unpaid balances.	76
	K111. Knowledge of ethical obligations regarding providing for continuation of treatment to the client.	76
	K112. Knowledge of ethical guidelines regarding the provision of therapeutic services when interacting with third-party payers.	79
	K47. Knowledge of referrals and resources to assist in meeting the needs of clients.	34

Task Statement	Knowledge Statement	Page
T48. Adhere to ethical guidelines regarding the acceptance of gifts and/or tokens of appreciation from clients.	K113. Knowledge of conditions/situations that may impair the integrity or efficacy of the therapeutic process.	77
	K114. Knowledge of ethical standards regarding the acceptance of gifts from clients.	77
T49. Adhere to ethical guidelines for protecting the welfare and dignity of participants when conducting research related to the provision of therapeutic services.	K115. Knowledge of procedures to safeguard participants when conducting research projects.	87
	K116. Knowledge of disclosures required to inform participants of the nature and role of research projects.	87
	K117. Knowledge of client rights regarding participation in research projects.	88
	K118. Knowledge of methods for protecting client confidentiality and data when conducting research projects.	88
T50. Address unethical or incompetent conduct of colleague by taking action to promote the welfare and interests of clients.	K119. Knowledge of conditions/situations that may impair the integrity or efficacy of the therapeutic process.	95
	K120. Knowledge of guidelines for addressing unethical or incompetent conduct of colleagues.	95
T51. Adhere to ethical guidelines for engaging in the supervisor/prelicensure practitioner relationship.	K121. Knowledge of ethical guidelines governing the supervisor/prelicensure practitioner relationship and responsibilities.	89

Notes

"AAMFT" stands for the American Association for Marriage and Family Therapy. "BBS" stands for Board of Behavioral Sciences. "BPC" stands for Business and Professions Code. "CAMFT" stands for the California Association of Marriage and Family Therapists.

[1] http://www.bbs.ca.gov/exams/exam_news.shtml
[2] If you really want to look it up, it's California BPC section 4980.02
[3] CAMFT Code of Ethics standard 3.6
[4] B. R. Benitez, "Guidelines for the treatment of minors," *The Therapist.*
[5] California BPC section 4982(v)
[6] M. Griffin, "On writing progress notes," *The Therapist.*
[7] By statute – California Penal Code section 11165.1(b), to be specific – this would be considered child abuse and would be a mandated report. However, the Department of Consumer Affairs (which oversees the BBS) issued a legal opinion in 2013 in response to my presentation to the BBS on the problems that result from this statutory requirement. The DCA opinion gives MFTs more latitude than the statute when it comes to reporting consensual oral sex, anal sex, or object penetration involving minors. Further efforts to clarify the law since then have failed, leaving the reporting requirements unclear. The BBS is aware of this concern, and as such is unlikely to include any test items that are related to this issue.
[8] National Children's Advocacy Center
[9] National Children's Advocacy Center
[10] American Psychological Association, *Elder abuse and neglect: In search of solutions.* National Committee for the Prevention of Elder Abuse, *What is elder abuse?* S. A. Salsbury, "Clinical brief: Recognizing, reporting, and responding to dependent adult abuse," *Topics in integrative health care: An integrative journal.*
[11] Named for its basis in law, which is California Welfare and Institutions Code section 5150
[12] A. Wellisch, "The 5150 foxtrot," *The Therapist.*
[13] D. Jensen, "Diagnosing a subpoena for validity," *The Therapist.*
[14] G. Corey, M. S. Corey, C. Corey, & P. Callanan, *Issues and Ethics in the Helping Professions, 9th ed.*
[15] AAMFT Code of Ethics standard 8.5

[16] A. Tran, "Third party reimbursement," *The Therapist.*
[17] CAMFT Code of Ethics standard 1.2
[18] AAMFT Code of Ethics standard 5.3
[19] AAMFT Code of Ethics standard 7.7
[20] BBS *Disciplinary Guidelines*
[21] BBS *Disciplinary Guidelines*
[22] CAMFT Code of Ethics standard 5
[23] CAMFT Code of Ethics standard 5.2
[24] CAMFT Code of Ethics standard 5.1